American Pickup Trucks
of the 1960s

Veloce

Also from Veloce:

Those Were The Days ... Series
Alpine Trials & Rallies 1910-1973 (Pfundner)
American 'Independent' Automakers – AMC to Willys 1945 to 1960 (Mort)
American Station Wagons – The Golden Era 1950-1975 (Mort)
American Trucks of the 1950s (Mort)
American Trucks of the 1960s (Mort)
American Woodies 1928-1953 (Mort)
Anglo-American Cars from the 1930s to the 1970s (Mort)
Austerity Motoring (Bobbitt)
Austins, The last real (Peck)
Brighton National Speed Trials (Gardiner)
British and European Trucks of the 1970s (Peck)
British Drag Racing – The early years (Pettitt)
British Lorries of the 1950s (Bobbitt)
British Lorries of the 1960s (Bobbitt)
British Touring Car Racing (Collins)
British Police Cars (Walker)
British Woodies (Peck)
Café Racer Phenomenon, The (Walker)
Don Hayter's MGB Story – The birth of the MGB in MG's Abingdon Design & Development Office (Hayter)
Drag Bike Racing in Britain – From the mid '60s to the mid '80s (Lee)
Dune Buggy Phenomenon, The (Hale)
Dune Buggy Phenomenon Volume 2, The (Hale)
Endurance Racing at Silverstone in the 1970s & 1980s (Parker)
Hot Rod & Stock Car Racing in Britain in the 1980s (Neil)
Last Real Austins 1946-1959, The (Peck)
Mercedes-Benz Trucks (Peck)
MG's Abingdon Factory (Moylan)
Motor Racing at Brands Hatch in the Seventies (Parker)
Motor Racing at Brands Hatch in the Eighties (Parker)
Motor Racing at Crystal Palace (Collins)
Motor Racing at Goodwood in the Sixties (Gardiner)
Motor Racing at Nassau in the 1950s & 1960s (O'Neil)
Motor Racing at Oulton Park in the 1960s (McFadyen)
Motor Racing at Oulton Park in the 1970s (McFadyen)
Motor Racing at Thruxton in the 1970s (Grant-Braham)
Motor Racing at Thruxton in the 1980s (Grant-Braham)
Superprix – The Story of Birmingham Motor Race (Page & Collins)
Three Wheelers (Bobbitt)

Truckmakers
DAF Trucks since 1949 (Peck)
Mercedes-Benz Trucks (Peck)

General
Automotive A-Z, Lane's Dictionary of Automotive Terms (Lane)
Chrysler 300 – America's Most Powerful Car 2nd Edition (Ackerson)
Chrysler PT Cruiser (Ackerson)
Dodge Challenger & Plymouth Barracuda (Grist)
Dodge Charger – Enduring Thunder (Ackerson)
Dodge Dynamite! (Grist)
Drive on the Wild Side, A – 20 Extreme Driving Adventures From Around the World (Weaver)
Dune Buggy Handbook (Hale)
Ford Cleveland 335-Series V8 engine 1970 to 1982 – The Essential Source Book (Hammill)
Ford F100/F150 Pick-up 1948-1996 (Ackerson)
Ford F150 Pick-up 1997-2005 (Ackerson)
Ford GT – Then, and Now (Streather)
Ford GT40 (Legate)
Ford Model Y (Roberts)
Ford Small Block V8 Racing Engines 1962-1970 – The Essential Source Book (Hammill)
Ford Thunderbird From 1954, The Book of the (Long)
France: the essential guide for car enthusiasts – 200 things for the car enthusiast to see and do (Parish)
Grand Prix Ford – DFV-powered Formula 1 Cars (Robson)
Jeep CJ (Ackerson)
Jeep Wrangler (Ackerson)
Land Rover Series III Reborn (Porter)
Land Rover, The Half-ton Military (Cook)
Micro Caravans (Jenkinson)
Micro Trucks (Mort)
Morgan 3 Wheeler – back to the future! The (Dron)
Motorhomes, The Illustrated History (Jenkinson)
N.A.R.T. – A concise history of the North American Racing Team 1957 to 1983 (O'Neil)
Nothing Runs – Misadventures in the Classic, Collectable & Exotic Car Biz (Slutsky)
Racing Line – British motorcycle racing in the golden age of the big single (Guntrip)
Renewable Energy Home Handbook, The (Porter)
Singer Story: Cars, Commercial Vehicles, Bicycles & Motorcycle (Atkinson)
Sleeping Beauties USA – abandoned classic cars & trucks (Marek)
Tatra – The Legacy of Hans Ledwinka, New Collector's Edition of 1500 copies (Margolius & Henry)
Two Summers – The Mercedes-Benz W196R Racing Car (Ackerson)
Volkswagen Bus Book, The (Bobbitt)
Volkswagen Bus or Van to Camper, How to Convert (Porter)
VW T5 Camper Conversion Manual (Porter)
VW Campers (Copping)
Which Oil? – Choosing the right oils & greases for your antique, vintage, veteran, classic or collector car (Michell)

Veloce Publishing's other imprints:

 A range of quality books about military history

 www.hubbleandhattie.com
A range of quality books dedicated to animal welfare

eBooks and Apps available from www.digital.veloce.co.uk

For post publication news, updates and amendments relating to this book please visit www.veloce.co.uk/books/V4803

www.velocebooks.com

First published in March 2016 by Veloce Publishing Limited, Veloce House, Parkway Farm Business Park, Middle Farm Way, Poundbury, Dorchester DT1 3AR, England. Fax 01305 268864 / e-mail info@veloce.co.uk / web www.veloce.co.uk or www.velocebooks.com. ISBN 978-1-845848-03-5; UPC 6-36847-04803-7.

Contents

Preface

This is the 13th motoring book I have had published along with my son Andrew. Once again, we have combined his photographic skills and my writing to tell the story this time about the *American ½-Ton Pickup Trucks of the 1960s.*

In the 1950s, pickup trucks had begun to evolve

Ford and Chevrolet pickups like these dominated the ½-ton pickup truck market during the 1960s, and set standards in reliability, rugged design, and hauling capability, but not always in innovation and styling. (N Mort Collection)

from being strictly utilitarian vehicles, built for hauling and the daily chores of farm life, to a more sophisticated, comfortable, performance oriented, and stylish vehicle, for use as a family transport vehicle as well.

By the 1960s the American pickup truck was playing an even greater role in the increasing entrepreneurship of the US middle class. More and more small businesses found the ½-ton pickup truck ideally suited for daily toil. At the same time, the continued boom in the building of roads, shopping centres and suburban homes in the burgeoning business climate of 1960s America, created a huge demand for these modern workhorses.

Today, these stylish and more comfortable dual-purpose work and family pickup truck designs are some of the favorites of American vintage truck collectors.

As well as my enthusiasm and fascination with these

American vehicles, and my son Andrew's photographic talents, this book would not have been possible without the encouragement, kindness and co-operation of many others.

Numerous collector car and truck dealers in Canada and the United States were very supportive of our project. This included Country Classic Cars, Hyman Motors Ltd and The Stable Ltd.

Bill Peeters of Bill's Truck Stop, and longtime International dealer and collector George Kirkham of Southland International Trucks Ltd, in particular, helped immensely by clarifying various facts and providing images.

Andrew and I would also like to thank Rod Grainger of Veloce Publishing for his encouragement and continuing faith in our endeavors.

Stylish pickups were all the rage in the 1960s, and American manufacturers responded by building a wider and wider range of interpretations of the traditional ½-ton truck. By 1969 and a decade of El Camino evolution, the lines between a traditional ½-ton pickup truck and a car were truly blurred. The El Camino had many of the positive attributes of a pickup truck, yet it still had a lot of automobile DNA. That proved to be both an asset and a drawback to the El Camino, as well as to its direct competitor – the Ford Ranchero. (N Mort Collection)

Introduction

American ½-ton Pickup Trucks of the 1960s examines the further evolution of these popular, highly practical and often very stylish vehicles throughout the decade, and includes numerous new alternative designs and engineering approaches.

Although still often purchased as a basic utility vehicle during the 1960s, there were more and more buyers looking for a stylish, comfortable, good handling and performing, lightweight pickup truck that could do double duty, too. The growth in popularity of camping, hunting and fishing during the decade was in part due to the ever-evolving American pickup truck.

This volume also focuses on specifications, industry facts and figures, and optional equipment through detailed text and previously unpublished images.

Also included is a chapter focusing on the details of five very different and distinctive American ½-ton pickup truck designs from this decade.

Such was the burgeoning popularity of pickups that, by 1964, Ford was building three very different ½-ton model trucks. These included its Econoline, the Ranchero, and the traditional F-100. The models were not just badge-engineered variants, but rather completely distinctive designs, created to fulfill the diverse needs of North American buyers. (N Mort Collection)

The continuation of the important role played by the lightweight, high production ½-ton pickup truck in American life during the 1960s is often overshadowed by its innate ruggedness, reliability and utilitarian nature. Yet, as the quickly changing 1960s evolved, so did the pickup truck – as did the manufacturers' interpretation of this increasingly popular vehicle.

The pickup truck models, and increased number of interpretations, continued the initial 1950s trend towards more style, comfort and optional equipment. Yet, in the 1960s, the pickup truck would less and less assume the lines and styling of its flashy sibling car versions, and instead take on an overall more unique identity and a character of its own.

In the 1960s the stigma of the farmer/country boy pickup was long gone. The pickup truck was everyday transportation that, on weekends could haul your trailer or boat, or fulfill other recreational needs. Although two-toning was not as popular as it was in the previous decade, it was still offered. By 1969 a vinyl-covered or imitation vinyl roof had become popular on cars. The treatment had provided a sportier 'convertible-look' to mundane, family four-door sedans, so it wasn't long before it was offered on pickup trucks, too, such as this 1969 Dodge D100 Adventurer ½-ton. (N Mort Collection)

The new decade

While the 1950s were almost revolutionary in terms of truck designs and philosophies, the 1960s were more evolutionary.

Pickup truck design, styling and marketing had gone through a complete rethink in the 1950s, compared to the 1940s. In the 1960s, the ½-ton American pickup truck was no longer just a farm or labour workhorse, it was now a practical family vehicle that was also used regularly for hauling household items, groceries and shopping, towing light trailers and family recreational equipment.

Each year brought more available comfort and convenience 'packages' offered by the manufacturers

By the late 1960s there was no social stigma attached to owning a pickup truck. Families and young couples owned pickup trucks to fulfill lifestyles that included boating, dirt bikes, fishing, camping, skiing – you name it. The 1960s was a 'youth market.' The baby boomers were determined to be 'cool' and live life to the fullest after growing up in the sober, overly conservative postwar years of the fifties, with atom bomb shelters, 'McCarthyism,' and the 'Cold War.' The latest pickup trucks or new 'sport pickups' helped provide that freedom, despite the horrendous ongoing events throughout the decade. (1968 Chevrolet C-10 featured.) (N Mort Collection)

and dealers, or available through specialty companies focusing on aftermarket alternative equipment.

The continuing prosperity in the United States and Canada in the sixties allowed families the opportunity to own more than one vehicle, and very often that additional vehicle would be a versatile ½-ton pickup truck.

Demand was such that American manufacturers offered more and more models, and a slew of new and exciting designs, such as a reinterpreted Ford Ranchero and Chevrolet El Camino, and the cab-forward Chevrolet Corvair 95, Dodge A-100 and Ford Econoline.

The prophetic 1964 lyrics written and sung by Bob Dylan stated: "The times they are a-changin' " – and that was true for everybody, including the American truck manufacturers.

Of all the decades in American history, the 1960s had one of the most profound influences on the American way of life. Philosophical changes in thinking and living occurred as a result of many social and political events, including the ongoing Cold War, the escalating war in Vietnam, the Communist threat, the assassination of Martin Luther King, Robert 'Bobby' Kennedy and President John F Kennedy, the racial riots, desegregation, the Kent State Shootings, peace and freedom marches, the hippie and peace movements, and the start of a cultural revolution.

All these 1960s events may not have directly

Another natural ½-ton pickup truck metamorphosis that took place in the final years of the 'Swinging Sixties' was the 'Sportrucks.' Designed for fun – including higher performance and almost sports car handling – the Sportrucks were outfitted in all the latest popular options, colors, fancy stainless trim and striping kits. In its advertising and brochures, Dodge repeatedly referred to its 1969 Dodge and Fargo ½-ton Sweptline D100s as 'Sportrucks.'
(N Mort Collection)

influenced ½-ton pickup truck buyers, but they did impact on all Americans (and Canadians, too, to a large degree).

While the US as a whole was fractionalizing into Doves and Hawks, equal rights activists versus growing racism, the majority of everyday Americans seemed to be enjoying life in the 'Swinging Sixties,' and going out and buying more higher-performance pickup trucks for sports, camping, fishing, hunting and the great outdoors.

Famed American author John Steinbeck wrote his travelogue novel *Travels with Charley: In Search of America*, which was published in 1962. It described an

The 1960s saw Ford, GM and Dodge all offering 4WD versions of their pickup trucks, and also expanding their line-ups of what was becoming the popular Sport-Utility market, based on the pickup truck frame and drivetrain. The longtime leader and pioneer in this market going into the 1960s was Jeep. Despite this, Kaiser-Jeep Corporation barely survived the decade. Early in 1970, American Motors Corporation was the new owner of Jeep. (N Mort Collection)

The sixties saw an attempt to reinvent the blossoming pickup truck market in North America. There were two very different approaches, with Ford and GM taking both of them, and Dodge one. Cab Forward pickup truck designs were introduced by the 'Big Three' in an attempt to expand their share of the lucrative market. Also, the car-based GM Chevrolet El Camino, and Ford's Ranchero were sold in full, intermediate and compact sizes, first stressing economy and then performance over the decade, in an attempt to find the right formula. The rubber burning '69 El Camino is pictured. (N Mort Collection)

Whereas the pickup trucks of the 1950s lend themselves to body customization, the 1960s pickups don't, due to their straighter, simpler lines. Customized sixties pickup trucks are usually 'mild' rather than 'wild,' and tend to be lowered and fitted with upgraded suspensions, wider, fancier wheels, better interiors, tonneau covers, and trick paintwork. (N Mort Collection)

Pickup trucks were also being promoted as 'seven days a week' vehicles for work and fun. Camping, hunting and fishing were very popular pastimes in the 1960s, and both dealers and the aftermarket suppliers offered lots of items to help buyers enjoy their hobbies using their pickup trucks. (N Mort Collection)

almost 10,000 mile road trip around the US in 1961. Steinbeck, along with his standard poodle 'Charley,' toured in his 1960 Chevy pickup camper truck, that he dubbed 'Rocinante.'* His findings were insightful and inspirational to thousands of Americans who read his book. They would follow his lead, and do the same in their pickup truck in the sixties.

Which brings us to yet another insightful quote,

taken from Charles Dickens' novel, *A Tale of Two Cities*, just over a century before, but which seems more than apropos for the 1960s. "It was the best of times, it was the worst of times ..."

*Steinbeck's 'Rocinante,' the pickup camper truck, is on display in the National Steinbeck Center gallery in Salinas, California.

TRANSISTOR RADIO   4-SPEED SYNCHRO-SHIFT TRANSMISSION   LOADFLITE AUTOMATIC TRANSMISSION (3-speed)   POWER STEERING

POWER BRAKES   HEATER & DEFROSTER—RECIRC. OR FRESH AIR   "SURE-GRIP" DIFFERENTIAL   INSIDE REAR VIEW MIRROR

OUTSIDE MIRROR—RIGHT SIDE—5" HEAD   CHROME FRONT BUMPER   WHEEL COVERS (15" wheels)   FULL-WIDTH REAR WINDOW

Annual automobile and truck production continued to steadily increase to record levels throughout the 1960s. At the same time, buyers desired more sophistication, luxury and convenience in their vehicles. As a result, there was a similar increase in the number of aftermarket specialty companies to meet these demands. A perfect example was the 1961 introduction by the James W Hartje Co, of a fiberglass cover for your Ranchero, El Camino, or other pickup truck beds. Available in a wide variety of sizes, the price was a reasonable $123.50 US. It was completely waterproof, could be easily locked, and installation necessitated drilling only four holes. (N Mort Collection)

Ford and Mercury

Ford drives 'tough' into the 1960s

Following WWII, Ford's all-new postwar 1948 'Bonus Built' trucks were offered in 139 variations, and were now known as the F-Series. These trucks helped Ford regain its market share, but more importantly put the entire company back on the road to prosperity.

In 1951 the 'Five Star Extra' option package was offered, which included chrome window and grille moldings, a foam-filled seat with two-tone trim, interior door trim panels, sound-deadening in the doors, floors and cab, an acoustic, insulated headliner, dual sun visors,

In 1961, '62 and '63, Ford's Styleside pickup trucks were promoted as "… exclusive one-piece cab-body for smarter looks, greater strength and a solid, fine-car feel," or so said a 1962 ad. As well as the smooth-looking Styleside, a traditional separate cab and box Flareside was available with the same Six or V8 power. These models were sold in Standard and Deluxe forms. Both had the same Standard brown vinyl interior, but the Deluxe's was a better vinyl that had a leather look. Other Deluxe features included a left-side armrest, coat hook, emblems, cowl/firewall insulation for noise reduction, and other minor amenities. (N Mort Collection)

armrests, horns, a cigarette lighter, a courtesy interior dome light, and a glovebox lamp. This Ford F1 upgrade 'Five Star Extra' option package began the industry trend toward building a more comfortable, widely optioned pickup truck. It also went on to help make the Ford F1 the top-selling pickup truck in North America since 1951.

A newly angular and sculptured F-100 was debuted in 1957. The design abandoned the traditional separate fenders front and rear, and there were no runningboards. The new cab design was fully integrated into the overall styling with the now standard 'Styleside' smooth-sided rear fenders and box. The new wide, smooth-sided, inside and out box was an important feature on Ford's pickup trucks, as it added approximately 45 percent more loading space. The traditional narrow box Flareside would continue to be offered, but relatively few were ordered.

By 1960 the four year old F-100 styling was beginning to show its age, despite its overall clean looks.

Ford's rivals began introducing their latest designs, yet there would be no plans for any dramatic styling changes for another six years.

Annual face-lifts were a regular task in the styling department, and for 1960 the F-100 received a larger, more intricate grille that incorporated the parking lights and a vented hood, along with the latest badging and minor trim changes.

Instead of cosmetic styling, Ford focused on engineering and industry-first innovations, to maintain its number one position in the ½-ton pickup truck market.

The 1960 Ford F-100 featured improved springs and beefier frame cross-members, a 10 percent more efficient heater, rubber door gaskets, as well as upgraded and simplified wiring throughout, and a better flow-through exhaust system.

The F-100 pickup's overall look remained relatively the same until 1967, in part due to its familiar paint schemes and wide, heavy-looking

In 1960, the usual changes to the hood and grille were utilized for a fresh look to start the new decade. A thick bar now connected the horizontal, dual headlamp pods which were larger in size and slanted inwards. Some felt it gave the F-100 an insect-like look. A rocket hood ornament was added, which was definitely a fifties styling holdover. For 1960, Ford's biggest news was offering factory four-wheel-drive on its F-100 ½-ton pickups. (N Mort Collection)

The 1960 Ford F-100 came in two wheelbases, with either the Styleside or Flareside box. The 110in wheelbase was fitted with a 6½ft box, while the 118in wheelbase version carried an 8ft box. Note on this example a much later style of hubcap is fitted on original wheels. Flareside production in 1960 reached 27,383 units, while the Styleside pickups totaled 113,875 trucks. (N Mort Collection)

horizontal grille, it was the wide accent arches on the fenders over the wheel openings that really dated the styling.

Yet, there was what Ford called a major restyling in 1961. It consisted of a new grille, as well as a return to single headlamps and an overall more rounded look. The F-100 cab was also completely revamped. The A-post was slanted forward, the rear window enlarged, and the entire greenhouse increased in size due to a higher roof. Overall, though, the 1961 Ford F-100 was lower and wider, with two longer wheelbases offered in 114in and 122in.

The major change was the integral cab and box. No longer separate, it provided a much smoother look and a slightly larger loadspace. It didn't allow for any flexing under load or on uneven road surfaces, though, and would also prove to be a rust prone design.

In the traditional pickup, when the truck's box got too rusty it was removed, and a platform was built on to continue to carry loads. With the integral box this wasn't possible. This design of the pickup box and rear fenders extending into the cab was a feature of the Styleside from 1961 to the end of the 1963 model year, when it was proving detrimental to sales.

After extensive changes in 1961, the 1962 F-100 remained virtually unchanged, other than the Ford name being moved above the grille.

For 1963 Ford offered both the integral design and a separate box on its Styleside models, along with the Flareside. Numerous minor changes were made, but overall only a new grille identified it as a 1963 F-100.

A further increase in comfort took place in 1964, when Ford offered factory air-conditioning for the first time on all its light-duty trucks. The biggest visual changes included a 1in higher roof, another new grille and lettering. These F-100s were also quieter, as four more pounds of insulation were added.

Then, in 1965, came the introduction of Ford's iconic 'Twin-I-Beam' front suspension on its F-Series trucks, which provided a smoother, more comfortable, yet rugged ride. The Twin-I-Beam suspension would continue to be a Ford feature for the next 25 years, and helped push overall light truck sales to over the 500,000 sales mark.

Visually little changed, it was the power that gave sales people lots to talk about, with three new engines being offered.

There were dramatic changes to the F-100 pickup's overall design in 1961. One of the changes made was only found on one of Ford's two ½-ton pickup models: two latches on the tailgate and hinged support arms replaced the standard industry chains on the Styleside, but interestingly, the Flareside retained the old latch and chain design. Engine choices in 1961 consisted of the 135hp, 223ci Six and the 160hp, 292ci V8. (N Mort Collection)

Mercury ½-ton pickups were also available in Canada with a 6½ or 8ft box. Here, a 1962 Styleside integral one-piece cab and box is featured. These models boasted one of the biggest load capacities in their class. The 6½ft box provided 65.1ft^3 of loadspace. When a buyer selected an 8ft box, that loadspace jumped to almost 80ft^3. (N Mort Collection)

This surviving 1963 Ford F-100 Styleside is a rarer sight today, having been built as an integral cab and box design. Most of these have rusted away over the decades. Starting in 1963, Ford again offered a separate box as an extra cost option, as more and more complaints were being voiced by potential buyers and owners. Size-wise, the integral box still offered some advantages, as it was about a ½in higher, 4in longer and 2in wider. (N Mort Collection)

In the final year of this F-100 bodystyle, 1966, Ford continued to focus on comfort. Outside, the grille was changed, but most of the improvements were inside the cab. Exterior colors consisted of red, green, blue, or beige, with color-keyed interiors.

A deluxe 'Ranger' edition featuring bucket seats, carpeting, a centre console, etc, was Ford's entry into the new sports truck market. Power steering and power brakes were optional, as were whitewall tires. Sales dropped slightly to 553,719 light-duty trucks.

Ford had continued to dominate the light-duty truck market, despite its aging design but 1967 brought an all-new F-100, with clean simple lines and straightforward styling, and flat sculptured sides with softly rounded corners. The hood was double walled, as was the Styleside's box. Both the hood and the rear tailgate were simple one-hand operations. The wider, redesigned cabs provided four more inches of

In 1963 Ford had not planned to offer a separate box on its integral cab-box Styleside. As a result no new box design was available, so Ford re-used its 1957-1960 Styleside box while it prepared new tooling for 1964. The more angular shape made it quite obvious it was an add-on.
(N Mort Collection)

This 1963 F-100 Flareside is fitted with the standard 6½ft box, but was also available with an 8ft box. The boxes could be ordered with either a wooden or steel floor, depending on the model. The Flareside came with a short runningboard between the cab and the rear fender to aid loading. A new grille design provided a fresher look. A fully-synchronized 3-speed transmission was introduced, yet shifting was made even smoother through repositioning of the brake and clutch pedals. (N Mort Collection)

The 1963 Flareside interior, whether on the Standard or Deluxe model, was very functional. Seating was made more comfortable, thanks to new synthetic foam cushions. A long list of available interior options also helped. These included a radio, a right-hand armrest and sunvisor, a fresh-air or recirculating-air heater, a tinted windscreen, turn signals, windshield washers, woven plastic trim, a chrome-trimmed instrument cluster, a white steering wheel with chrome horn ring, a cigar lighter, and more. (N Mort Collection)

In 1964 Ford introduced its new longer 128in wheelbase for its F-100 Flareside ½-ton and Styleside pickups with the 8ft box. The short box (6½ft) was mounted on the 114in wheelbase versions. Ford noted the new longer wheelbase provided even greater stability, improved weight distribution, better handling and a smoother ride, but it was also to cash-in on the camper applications becoming popular with pickup truck owners and their families. The Flareside came with a wooden floor while the new separate Styleside box had a steel floor. A one-handed centre latch graced the new separate box. (N Mort Collection)

The 'Driverized Cabs' in 1964 featured color-keyed interiors for greater style. More importantly, though, a new, optional, six-cylinder engine provided, as Ford said: "... V8 hustle with six-cylinder economy." The 262ci Six provided excellent fuel economy, yet had more torque. The old Fordomatic was replaced by a heftier Cruise-O-Matic transmission, but it was not available with the new Six. (N Mort Collection)

Once again for 1965, there were few styling changes made to the F-100/Mercury 100 pickups other than the grille and badging. Yet, under the hood you had new choices, ranging from a standard, 150hp, 240ci Six; an optional 170hp, 300ci Six; or a 208hp, 352ci V8. And then, there was Ford's new and much hailed independent front suspension. (Andrew Mort)

shoulder room, with a more comfortable 3in wider seat. The instrument panel was described as being 'swept-away' in shape which allotted even more room inside the cab. The cargo boxes were the same 6½ft and 8ft sizes. The new F-Series also featured improved visibility and additional car-like conveniences, such as reversible keys, keyless locking, higher capacity cowl ventilation, and standard two-speed wipers. F-100 sales saw Flareside top 18,000, while nearly 205,000

In 1965 the combination of new engines and Ford's sensational Twin I-beam suspension helped Ford break a new light truck production record totaling 563,137 units. Also, Ford had benefited with its new Camper Special Packages, now available on an F-100 or M100 129in wheelbase. (Andrew Mort)

By the mid-sixties, camping and pickup trucks were becoming synonymous. This 1966 Ford pickup was fitted with a fiberglass camper unit, whereas some were fitted with aluminum units. Smaller caps* could also be used daily for work, to keep items safely locked away and out of sight. *The term 'cap' was used to refer to a hardtop, cab-height fitting that enclosed the entire rear box, with access via the tailgate. (N Mort Collection)

This 1968 Ford pickup was fitted with a family-size fiberglass camper unit, and offered as the First Prize by *Motor Trend*'s sister publication, *Wheels Afield*. The popularity of the great outdoors, and using a pickup truck as a motorhome to go anywhere and sleep in, while camping, fishing, hunting or hiking, resulted in an increase in demand for more State and Provincial parks in the US and Canada. (N Mort Collection)

Camping was at its peak in 1969 as a popular way to vacation, and Ford had always been a leader in this field with both its trucks and station wagons. Advertised as a way of enjoying, playing and living in the great outdoors, Ford's Camper Specials could be ordered with all the heavy-duty components built in. Ford's long-touted Twin-I-Beam front suspension, we were told, "... smooths every mile along the way." (N Mort Collection)

Styleside ½-tons were sold. In addition to that there were chassis and cab and 4x4 F-100 sales of over 5000 more units.

Being all-new, the 1968 F-100 was treated only to the annual new grille, emblems, and change in marker and parking lights. The camper craze continued as more and more ½-ton pickups were being used as work vehicles through the week and mobile homes on the weekends.

Similar minor changes were made in 1969 as the decade came to an end.

A stereo/tape player, tinted glass, and full carpeting were popular F-Series options in 1969, due to the ever-increasing demand for greater everyday comfort and convenience. A minor change in the grille design and trim was about all that was new on the exterior. (N Mort Collection)

Mercury

Although Mercury continued to offer its own version of the F-100 in the 1960s, this was just badge engineered, and it differed only slightly in standard equipment, color and options offered.

Ford of Canada ended all Mercury truck production in 1968, yet, at that time, was offering close to 280 different Mercury truck models in all sizes.

The Mercury Series 100 ½-ton Flareside featured a separate body and box, and was also offered in factory four-wheel-drive form like its Ford counterpart, for plowing through mud, sand, gravel or deep snow, and could easily climb steep grades. (N Mort Collection)

Chevrolet and GMC

A new decade and a new Chevrolet and GMC ½-ton pickup truck. For 1960 these trucks got an all-new cab inside and out, a new frame, and a redesigned suspension. There was the C-series (Conventional) ½-tons, and the K-series (four-wheel-drives).

The front end of the new cab sported jet-like intakes protruding from the top of each fender. A wrap-around windscreen and full back window (optional), with narrow B-pillars, provided excellent all-round vision. The rounded look of the 1955-59 'Task Force' pickups was gone, yet with enough curved and carved styling cues to avoid being overly boxy.

Flat sculptured sides provided a sleek, trim look, as did the fact that the overall height was 7in lower.

A lower truck not only meant easier ingress and egress, but also improved handling and cornering.

The fact that the hood covered the tops of the front fenders allowed for more accessibility and easier servicing. The Fleetside models could be ordered with an 8½ft box. Both the Fleetside and Stepside had seal-tight tailgates for carrying grain. Interestingly, this 1960 Chevrolet Apache Stepside is all-original, with just 6000 miles on the odometer. (Andrew Mort)

GMC production had always constituted only a fraction of Chevrolet's truck numbers, yet the brand had a strong, loyal following. This particular 1960 GMC was rare, in that it was powered by the all-new V6. Improved ride and handling in 1960 were due to the new A-arm independent front suspension with ball joints and torsion bars. In the rear coil springs, control arms and repositioned shock absorbers, along with a stabilizer bar, greatly enhanced the ride. An added cross-member to the new ladder frame also improved rigidity. (N Mort Collection)

COMFORT-KING CABS

CHOICE OF V8 OR 6 CYLINDER ENGINES

SELECTED-WOOD FLOORS ON PICK-UPS AND PANELS

RUGGED REAR AXLE

CUSTOM COMFORT CUSHION OPTION

ENGINEERED REAR SUSPENSION

SURE STOP BRAKES

STURDY TWIST RESISTANT FRAME

CHOICE OF RUGGED TRANSMISSIONS

INDEPENDENT FRONT SUSPENSION

LOOK INTO CHEVROLET TODAY!

"Look Into Chevrolet Today" was seen as a clever advertisement in 1961, with a cutaway drawing used to highlight standard and optional features. Some appear to be somewhat obvious – one would hope the rear suspension was engineered, the frame was twist resistant and the brakes would stop your truck. Two-toning remained popular. Chevy engine choices were the 135hp, 235ci Six, a 150hp or 160hp, 283ci V8. (N Mort Collection)

Despite the trim looks, the interior was bigger and more comfortable.

Under the hood there were few changes on the Chevrolet models with the standard 135hp, 235ci Six or economy option 110hp Six on the C-10 Series. The 283ci V8 was a popular option. In contrast, GMC in 1960 was powered by an all-new 150hp, 304.7ci V6 with 260lb-ft torque at 1600-2000rpm.

The standard Chevrolet ½-ton was called a 'Deluxe,' and the upgraded model with more chrome and other features a 'Custom.' An 'Apache 10' nameplate was on the side of the Chevy front fender.

For 1961 there were few external changes, other than the front grille, and now fresh air through the front pods helped cool the engine. The economy Six was dropped.

The following year a more dramatic face-lift saw the Chevrolet and GMC pickup's jet-pods disappear in favor of parking lights. Two central, horizontal vents were added on the Chevy, and a single long vent on the GMC. While GMC maintained its quad lighting, Chevrolet went to single headlamps.

In 1963 there were the usual minor grille and trim changes to freshen the look, along with a redesigned front bumper that would be carried through into 1966.

The big news was a redesign of the formerly acclaimed independent front suspension. The expensive-to-build torsion bar system had gone, in favor of coil springs on all of GM's light-duty trucks. This allowed GM to remove the cross-member to build a less expensive ladder frame, and move to a two-stage rear coil spring suspension. The old coil spring system had caused unloaded pickups to dig themselves in on soft sand and in snow.

The venerable 235ci Six was replaced by a newly

While Fleetside sales easily dominated the market by 1963, the traditional Stepside pickup truck still provided loading advantages, not to mention being less prone to dings and dents if leading a hard life. As well as a usual 6½ft and 8ft box, you could order an even longer 9ft. All the boxes had hardwood floors and metal skid strips. (N Mort Collection)

designed 230ci 'High Torque' or 292ci six-cylinder engine. Light truck sales increased by 10.2 percent in 1963.

In 1964, the wrap-around windscreen was replaced by a curved glass set into canted-forward A-posts.

These changes, along with new trim and a reworked grille resulted in a very pleasing update in styling.

Inside was a redesigned dash, fresh materials and an overall dressier cab, while under the hood there was more horsepower. For the ½-ton Chevs the power increases resulted in a 140hp, 230ci Six, a 170hp, 292ci Six and a 175hp, 283ci V8. GMC had its standard 165hp, 305 V6, or optional 120hp, 230ci Six borrowed

Chevrolet was building a full range of trucks, and it was important to remind customers of this fact in its advertising, and also to show that every Chevrolet truck shared the same unique front end styling, whether it be the 1964 Fleetside C10 ½-ton Pickup, the C80 chassis-cab, or the Suburban Carryall with four-wheel-drive. Most Chevrolet advertising in the mid-1960s included more than one of its trucks. (N Mort Collection)

Advertised as "The Long Strong Line For '65," Chevrolet pointed out it had 18 models in its pickup truck line-up, including Fleetside, Stepside and four-wheel-drives. "All are available in a variety of body lengths, and payload ratings to suit your requirements." (N Mort Collection)

Although the Chevrolet Fleetside pickups were far more popular, the Stepside still commanded a substantial segment of the market. For '66, a more powerful 150hp, 250ci Six and the 220hp, 327ci V8 helped in this respect. In its last year with this bodystyle, GMC – and its bigger sibling Chevrolet – stressed its positive design elements. Interestingly, one design feature noted on the 1966 GMC models was four headlights, and not two like most pickups – including Chevrolet. Yet, the all-new for '67 GMC ½-ton pickups would be fitted with two headlamps. (N Mort Collection)

from Chevrolet, due in part to owner's complaints about the V6.

And, while color, flash, sex and image were important advertising tools in promoting a pickup truck in the 1960s, there were always the customers that just wanted the facts, as reassurance they were buying the toughest, most reliable truck on the market. Chevrolet knew this, and often placed info ads in magazines such

This one looks so good and is built so well you can use it for almost anything!

The 1967 GMC and Chevrolet ½-ton pickup trucks were dramatically changed in both appearance and construction. The old styling nuances had gone, as this was a clean, smooth, 'form follows function' look. It was lower and sleeker in appearance. New body construction was employed, with fewer welds and an all-steel pickup box. The cab was also roomier with improved visibility. A dual master brake cylinder system was a standard safety feature. (N Mort Collection)

as *Life* and *Look,* that were common reading in waiting rooms and outer offices. These ads stressed body and frame construction, suspension features, engine availability, and model ranges.

The changes for 1965 on both the Chevrolet and GMC pickups was basically badging. The only real news was the optional factory air-conditioning and power steering.

In its last Series year, the changes were kept to a minimum, apart from a couple of new engine choices. Both Chevrolet and GMC got the same in-line six-cylinder engine upgrade. The GMC 351.2ci V6 was now rated at 220hp which was better than many of the V8s offered in the light-duty truck market.

All new in 1967, Chevrolet was ready to go bumper to bumper with the equally new Ford F-100.

Being all-new last year, in '68, Chevrolet stood pat on most things, and once again stressed that the new Chev and GMC ½-ton pickup trucks had a solid, strong body and separate frame construction. Double-walled construction could be found in the cab roof, cowl, windshield pillars, and door openings, and, in the Fleetside models, body/box side panels. The exterior panels had no external weld joints, and the front fenders were fitted with liners, which provided greater rust resistance. (N Mort Collection)

The 1968 Chevrolet and GMC 910 ½-ton pickup, as seen here, featured coil springs at all four wheels for a smoother ride, and provided an independent front suspension. Chevrolet boasted its 250ci Six was the biggest standard Six in any 'leading' make. The larger 292ci Six was optional, as were four V8s. (N Mort Collection)

Chevrolet would never get away with ad copy like this today, and must have agitated and helped fuel the feminist movement. Following the line "A Chevy pickup is built to be woman-handled" the copy got worse by stating, "Don't get us wrong. Mankind's favorite truck is as tough as ever." If that wasn't enough, the advertisement went on to say, "But the '69 Chevy has womankind in mind, too," by touting the smooth ride, soft molded seats, power steering, and air-conditioning, and concluded with, "It's enough to make the grade with any gal ..." (N Mort Collection)

Touted by Chevrolet as having the "... most significant cab and sheet metal styling changes in Chevrolet history," the new Sweptline and Stepside were designed to be stylish as well as ruggedly functional.

Sports trucks with higher performance and a growing youth market were becoming popular, and GM answered with its own interpretations. The new Chevrolet Custom Sports Truck featured a CST option that included special badging, bucket seats, a combination centre console/seat, chrome front bumper, horn button and dash knobs, bright pedal trim, an anodized grille, bright front end trim parts, and with the

option of the 220hp, 327ci V8. A total of 288,356 C-10 trucks were built in 1967.

Minor grille and trim changes were made in 1968, but side marker lights on front and back fenders were mandated by the government. The standard Chevrolet engine was the 155hp, 250ci Six with an optional 170hp, 292ci Six and a choice of three V8s. This included a 200hp, 307ci, and the 220hp, 327ci V8.

1969 saw a fresh grille design, taller hood, interior improvements, and new options that included additional option packages. A new 255hp, 350ci V8 was added in 1969 that would go on to become a legend, no matter what hood it sat under.

Although there was no new body styling in 1969, the Chevrolet C10 was treated to a more massive grille and higher hood line, for an all over bolder look. Improved body mounts provided a quieter, smoother ride, as did the new two-stage rear multi-leaf springs. Mandatory side marker lights replaced the previous reflectors. The new 350ci V8 was introduced to meet the needs of those hauling campers, as much as those hauling heavier cargo loads. The 310hp, 4-bbl, 396ci V8 was also available, but that was more to please the growing 'sport truck' market. (Andrew Mort)

Inside, numerous small, but important, improvements were seen in 1969. Seat and door panel materials were upgraded, and, for safety, the knobs on the dash were flatter, and the ignition recessed. A foot-operated brake was also fitted, to fall in line with current trends. (Andrew Mort)

The GMC's grille, trim and badging continued to be the key visual overall difference between it and the comparable Chevrolet pickup. A custom repaint could make a small businessman's pickup truck not only a mobile advertising tool, but also an attractive and artistic statement, as is the case with this 1969 GMC. (N Mort Collection)

Dodge and Fargo

The Dodge brothers began building trucks in Detroit in 1916, but in the early 1920s both brothers died. The company was eventually purchased in 1927 by the three-year-old Chrysler Corporation, to become its Dodge Division.

Dodge trucks continued to sell well over the decades, and would prove to be of reliable and rugged construction, not only on North American roads, but later on the battlefields of Europe.

Following WWII, fresh designs were introduced in 1948, including its all-new B-Series ½-ton pickup. Dodge's familiar 'Job-Rated' slogan was once again used in promotions.

Dodge continued to compete in the truck market with an ever increasing line-up, and in late 1954 an all-new C-1-Series cab and frame ½-ton pickup design was unveiled. It was continually updated, yet apart from sheet metal changes from 1957 through to 1960, Dodge trucks remained the same.

Still, Dodge pickup trucks excelled through the styling genius of Virgil Exner, who had taken over styling in 1955, and by 1957 had incorporated his 'Forward Look,' which was described as being 'Straight out of tomorrow.'

The good-looking Sweptside was dropped in January 1959, in favor of an all-new, even more upscale Sweptline, with its cab-wide box. The fins were gone, to be replaced by a squared-off, flat-sided, plain box.

Changes to the ½-ton pickup truck were limited to a new grille, badges and script. The big changes would occur in the 1960s.

For 1961 the all-new Dodge/Fargo line of pickup trucks was fitted with the equally all-new Slant six-cylinder engine. It would prove to be a rugged, fuel efficient and reliable powerplant, loved by both truck and automobile owners. The wheelbases grew from 108in to 114in, and from 116in to 122in. The floor of the new 'Driverized' cab was 3in lower, and, when combined with the new frame and cab, was a remarkable 7in lower overall. The cab was also 4in wider, and thus roomier. (N Mort Collection)

While 1960 was a year of change in the new medium- and heavy-duty trucks, the light-duty trucks soldiered on. The C-Series cab, first seen in 1955 models, remained, and, surprisingly, continued on the larger trucks until the mid-seventies, when Dodge abandoned those segments of the market.

The 1960 Dodge Sweptline remained one of the more stylish ½-tons on the market, despite the fact that little changed other than a revised grille, a soundproof headliner added inside, and an improved heavy-duty 3-speed transmission. Still, ½-ton sales increased to 33,179 units.

It was 1961 when Dodge and Fargo introduced the totally new R-series ½-ton pickup truck known as the 'Dart.' The name had been borrowed from Dodge's car line and, not surprisingly, lasted just one year. It made little sense to borrow the name in the first place, other than to qualify the division's 1961 advertising slogan of, 'Hauls like a truck, handles like the family car.'

Regardless of the name, the new Dodge was a winner, with fresh styling, a thoroughly modern frame, suspension and steering system. Plus, new for the truck line, was the tilted 30-degree, OHV, 225 Slant six-cylinder engine. A more economical 170ci version of this Slant Six was an option on the D100 ½-ton.

The larger, but lower, cab also had a larger greenhouse, which included a wider rear window. The wide flat hood, stately egg-crate grille, and dual headlamps provided a solid, modern look.

In 1963 Dodge and Fargo made only a few changes to their ½-ton pickup trucks throughout the year. In 1962 Dodge management, based on a 3-year study, had decided to abandon annual model changes in its truck lines. Instead, Dodge would simply upgrade its trucks through the year to stay up-to-date in the market, or out-do the competition. In 1963, the $9.00 price increase was, in reality, more than $13.00 worth of standard additions, which included an oil filter. This idea seemed to be working, as sales in 1963 reached 110,987 trucks. (N Mort Collection)

The Utiline and Sweptline were offered in Standard or Custom models, and the list of features was impressive. While the box length remained at 6½ and 8ft, the width was stretched by 4in, and thus increased the overall loadspace. Two-toning remained popular on these new trucks, and the novel push-button LoadFlite automatic transmission continued to be optional.

One engineering advance in 1961 was the redesigned steering geometry, now located behind the axle, which reduced effort by a remarkable 60 percent.

Overall, the bad year in the truck industry saw production drop 5.9 percent, Dodge sales were additionally hurt by the introduction of the Ford and Chevrolet compact pickups, as well as a plant strike.

Changes in 1962 were minimal, both inside and out, on all Dodge's truck lines, yet sales increased 48.1 percent to 96,102 units. Nearly 70 percent of those trucks were powered by a Six.

With a no annual model change policy in effect, the 1963 Dodge ½-ton pickups went virtually unaltered other than a $9.00 US price increase.

Little was changed initially in 1964, until April, when a new, black striped, 'Custom Sports Special' truck option arrived in Dodge showrooms, with an attention grabbing 365hp, 426ci V8 (not a Hemi) available.

In April 1965, new front end styling was introduced

In 1964 Dodge offered a Custom Sport Special option outfitted with the standard 225ci Six, but, more importantly, available with the optional 318ci or 426ci V8. Standard were bucket seats and a centre console complete with ashtray, cigarette lighter, map light and additional storage, as well as full carpeting, two armrests and sunvisors, racing stripes, a chrome front bumper, grille, and roof moldings. Optional equipment included tinted glass, a radio, and more. The 8ft Sweptline box was standard, but the Utiline version with a 7ft box was optional. (N Mort Collection)

A few changes were made that differentiated the 1965 Dodge and Fargo ½-ton pickups from their predecessors. A new, full-width grille provided a fresh and far more contemporary look, and the headlamps appeared much larger, thanks to dinner plate-sized aluminum bezels. Full length, wide, bright trim with a contrasting color insert also helped to alter overall appearance, as can be seen on this Fargo D100 Sweptline. (N Mort Collection)

Although the same cab was fitted to the late-arriving restyled 1965 D100 Utiline (114in wheelbase shown), the traditional rear fenders resulted in a more dated look overall. Still, it allowed for an unobstructed loadspace. Runningboards were fitted to ease side loading. The model could be ordered with a 6½ or 8ft box, both of which featured seasoned hardwood floors with steel skids. (N Mort Collection)

For 1967 Dodge continued to offer three different ½-ton models, and the standard D100 Sweptline and Utiline pickups were again offered on 114in and 128in wheelbases. The usual grille, trim and badge changes were made to the 1967 models. The A100 pickups, first introduced in 1964, continued to be offered basically unchanged. In the background, is a rarely-seen, optional, two-tone version. Restorers today tend to favor the two-tone look. (N Mort Collection)

The 1967 D100 Dodge and Fargo pickups could be ordered with the standard 140hp, 225ci Slant Six, the optional 210hp, 318ci V8, or the higher performance optional 258hp, 383ci V8. The A100 ½-ton pickup came as standard with a smaller 101hp, 170ci Slant Six, while the 140hp, 225ci Slant Six, and 210hp, 318ci V8 were optional. The Slant Six engines became legendary over the years for rugged dependability. (N Mort Collection)

which included a full-width grille, single rather than dual headlamps, and full-length trim moldings. An important design feature was the additional full, double wall construction on its Sweptline boxes. The competition was offering this already, but only the bottom two-thirds of the box. A bigger, one-hand-only tailgate, and trimmer tail lamps were other design and styling improvements.

Inside was a redesigned dash, and the pushbutton transmission was dropped in favor of a traditional column shifter.

Calendar production and annual model sales increased to record highs of 143,452 and 116,639, respectively.

1966 brought few changes for new model introductions, other than different colors, and a new transmission better suited for camper pickups. Such

was the popularity of camping in North America that aftermarket firms were even offering camper bodies for the compact A-100 pickups.

More and more optional packages were offered in 1967 to improve comfort, performance and usability. Visually no changes were made, but the 426ci V8 was no longer available as an option. Just the 318ci and now the 383ci V8 were offered.

There were cosmetic changes in 1968, with a new grille, and a move to vertical parking lights. The 'Custom Sports Special' was replaced by an even more stylish 'Adventurer' model. Total production for the model year was a record 183,015 light-duty trucks, that included the A-100 line, the ½-ton, ¾-ton, 1-ton and Power Wagon trucks in 2WD and 4WD.

The 1969 Utiline design provided a runningboard for easier loading and unloading of cargo. Dodge could claim it was the lowest-priced ½-ton pickup truck in America in 1969. The D100 – and the D200 – came with a new 'Cushion-Beam Suspension.' The '69 Dodge ½-tons also featured a new hood and side trim, plus the now mandatory front fender, side safety marker lights. Bucket seats were optional on all models. A total of 165,133 were built. (N Mort Collection)

For 1969 the Utiline pickup box was available in three lengths: 6½, 8 or 9ft. The boxes had a seasoned hardwood floor with steel skid strips with stake pockets on each side, so could be enclosed if required. There was a choice of three engines ranging from the 225 Slant Six to the 318ci V8, with a high performance 383ci V8 available for heavy loads, or just more fun in these 'muscle car' years. For the first time, V8 sales (103,288) exceeded six-cylinder sales (71,266 units). (N Mort Collection)

The 1969 Adventurer pickups were offered on a 114in or 128in wheelbase, and had a choice of three different engines, and three transmissions. Dress-up features included paint stripes, a bright finish grille, wheel lip, drip rail, hood-mounted turn indicators, gas cap, nameplates, sill and windshield moldings. There was a choice of five color interiors, including carpeting and fiberglass door panels. Other interior niceties included courtesy lights, a foam core headliner, and a cigar lighter. (N Mort Collection)

As the decade ended, no styling changes were made for 1969, though, finally, Dodge buyers got an improved front suspension. 'The Dude' was the new model for the youth market, with a black or white C-stripe on the side and other graphics, but still Dodge sales declined by around 10,000 units. Despite this, 1969 was still Dodge's second best year ever.

Fargo

Fargo trucks were introduced by Chrysler in 1928 as its Fleet Sales organization, and used in Canada as well as for Canadian exports around the world. Fargo trucks were, in the main, identical to Dodge trucks, except for nameplates and different cosmetic trim. The Fargo nameplate would also be used on some Commer vehicles after Chrysler had assumed control of the British Rootes Group.

In Canada the Fargo nameplate was dropped in 1972, but continued in Africa, the Middle East, Scandinavia, and elsewhere.

Fargo trucks were never marketed in the United States, nor were the Dodge clone DeSoto trucks, which were built for export markets only, and sold until that Division was dropped altogether by Chrysler in 1960. DeSoto ½-ton pickups were assembled and sold in Brazil, Australia, India, South Africa and Mexico, as well as Turkey, where local production continued past 1960.

Both Dodge and Fargo shared the Adventurer name. Standard safety features on all ½-tons were seatbelts, padded sun visors, dash and instrument panel, and an energy absorbing steering column fitted with a recessed steering wheel. Advertizers, who were always quick to use current colloquialisms, stated in the 1969 brochure: "Have a 'sit-in' at your Dodge or Fargo dealers." (N Mort Collection)

Studebaker, International and Jeep

Studebaker

In 1960 a fully restyled Studebaker ½-ton pickup truck was introduced, named the 'Champ.' Its Studebaker Lark front end styling, with the prominent rectangular grille, was well ahead of its time, considering the look of the latest Dodge Ram and Ford F-150s over the past decade or more.

The Standard, lower-priced, pickup was immediately identifiable by its painted hubcaps, grille, headlamp bezels, side vents and gas cap. These items were all in chrome or stainless on the Deluxe models. Other upmarket 'Deluxe' exterior features included fender moldings and bright metal window trim.

Other Champ ½-ton options included dual horns, a Caravan top, a painted rear bumper, a right-hand taillight, license plate frames, a locking gas cap, left and right exterior rearview mirrors, or extension left and right exterior rearview mirrors, a spotlight, directional signals, tinted glass, a right, rear fender kit for the spare tire, and more.

Inside, the new 1960 DeLuxe Champ model came with a padded dash, two sun visors, two armrests, a dome light and a sliding rear window.

Other optional 'period' luxuries included a clock, a Climatizer heater/defroster, seatbelts, a Kleenex dispenser, cigarette lighter, and dual door locks.

The foam rubber, vinyl-covered bench seat provided transport for up to three people. The cab was sound and heat insulated.

The chassis was all truck – not just Studebaker Lark, and was available in both ½-ton and ¾-ton guise.

The pickups were designated the SE5, SE6, SE7, SE11 and SE12 models. Standard power for the Champ was Studebaker's 90hp, 169ci Six in the SE5, but there were four engine choices in total. The SE6 and SE11 were powered by the larger 118hp, 245.6ci six L-head engine.

Studebaker added the Lark's polished stainless front fender trim to its new 1960 Champ pickup. Many Studebaker fans felt the use of the Lark bodywork gave the new Champ the old 1930s Coupe Express-look that was once so popular. As well as a pickup truck, you could also order your Champ in a stake and platform version, or in a heftier, ¾-ton size. (N Mort Collection)

The new cab was a cut-off at the B-pillar Lark body of a four-door sedan. It featured a slightly larger truck grille and heavier bumper. While this 'T cab was new, the box was carried over from the previous Scotsman pickup model, and the wheelbase remained the same at 122in. Also available were the standard T4 cab or a 'Deluxe' version known as the T6. (N Mort Collection)

The heavy-duty 180hp 259ci V8, or 210hp, 289ci V8 were also available as extra cost options, or the former was standard if you ordered the SE7 or SE12 models.

A 3-speed, manual sliding gear transmission was standard with a column shift. Options included the Flightomatic automatic transmission on the SE7 and SE12, or a four-speed manual transmission, and overdrive. Four-wheel hydraulic brakes were standard equipment.

More mechanical options included twin-traction, hill-holder, and power brakes. The lower sitting Champ pickups benefited from less drag, and thus returned better fuel economy than the previous taller models.

Studebaker advertised its Champ as being ideal for "You businessmen, hunters and fishermen, farmers, cattlemen, contractors, club managers and boat owners ... go to your Studebaker dealer this week, and try out that nimble new Champ for yourselves. You'll want to drive it right on home!"

Steel strikes and production delays resulted in a late introduction in the spring of 1960. As a result sales suffered. Adding to this slow start, it soon became apparent that the Lark cab design was prone to rust.

In 1961 to help encourage sales there were minor mechanical changes made, and cosmetically the front fender trim was raised. The standard 170ci six-cylinder now featured overhead valves, and there was a wider Spaceside box. Sales soon faltered again when problems with cracked valve seats were reported in the new six-cylinder engine, and an obvious dealer apathy towards the Champ didn't help either.

Although the Lark front end styling changed in 1961, and again in 1962, Champ pickups retained the same basic 1959-60 styling cues.

Minimal additional changes took place in 1962. The front fender trim was lowered once again to where it was in 1960, and the Flightomatic automatic transmission was now offered as an option on the six-cylinder models. The Spacesaver box was made standard in 1962.

In 1962 Champ sales increased, partly due to its lowest in the marketplace $1870 price tag. This base model offered a six-cylinder engine, a 6½ft box, and a 5000lb GVW.

The '63 Champ had improved steering, new swing-style brake and clutch pedals, 'sea-leg' front shock absorbers, and wider and longer front springs. Also made standard was a flow-through oil filter and numerous other features, while air-conditioning was added to the option list.

The SE would be the last pickup truck offered by Studebaker.

There was a 1964 Studebaker Champ built in the

The foam rubber, vinyl-covered bench seat provided accommodation for up to three people. The seat was covered in a smart emboss-pleated upholstery. The cab was also sound and heat insulated. (N Mort Collection)

An opening, two-piece, sliding rear window was quite a novel idea for 1960. Studebaker was one of the first truck manufacturers to offer this feature. Studebaker noted it was designed "... for the utmost in cooling ventilation during hot weather." (N Mort Collection)

Studebaker advertisements described the new Champ as "... handsome to look at, a pleasure to ride in, and fun to drive! ... and the Champ handles like a convertible." Yet, in the 1960s the new 'family car look' didn't prove to be as popular as it would be 40 years later. (N Mort Collection)

Studebaker stressed in its promotional material, "You businessmen, hunters and fishermen, club managers and boat owners ... go to your Studebaker dealer this week, and try out the nimble new Champ for yourselves. You'll want to drive it right on home!" Yet, it was also subtly suggested through brochure and magazine advertisements that women, too, were quite comfortable driving its new Champ. In the 1960s this chauvinistic attitude was very common. (N Mort Collection)

By 1963 the decisions had been made about which models would continue to be built in Canada with Studebaker's main plant closing in South Bend. The 1963 Champ pickup trucks were visually identical from the outside to the 1962 Champs in their last full year of production. Total production of all of Studebaker's trucks from ½-ton to 2-ton had increased slightly in 1962, to 8742 units. In the 1963 calendar year, sales increased yet again to 13,117 units before truck production ceased forever. (N Mort Collection)

International Harvester noted in its 1960 B-Series ads, "They're ruggedly designed for truck work … sold right by truck-trained men … serviced economically at convenient dealer and branch points all over the map." Often the pickup truck ads would picture one of its bigger 'Conventional' or 'COE' brethren, in what International Harvester boasted as the "World's Most Complete Line" of trucks. (N Mort Collection)

fall of 1963, and it remained available on dealer lots until the end of civilian pickup truck production in South Bend on December 27th.

At that point all Studebaker production ceased in South Bend, Indiana, and all automobile manufacturing was transferred to the Hamilton, Ontario, Canada plant.

Studebaker sold the rights to the Avanti sports coupe to Nate Altman of South Bend in 1964, and he also secured the rights to the Champ and larger Transtar trucks. While Altman went on to build the Avanti, the light trucks were never put back into production by the new Avanti Motor Corporation.

International

A time of prosperity, the 1960s as a decade would see many changes in the trucking industry as a whole.

By 1960 there were very few truck manufacturers around that could lay claim to being a century old, but

In its last year before a complete redesign, the International B110 was advertised as the "true-truck," by offering the V-266ci V8, 304ci V8 or 345ci V8 engine as standard equipment, Bonus-Load bodies of up to 8½ft provided 25 percent more cargo space, more cab glass area, and extra insulation in the floors and doors. The Black Diamond 220ci and 240ci Six was a special order. It was the second year for the B-Series, with its quad headlamps, egg crate grille, and bigger, wider cargo box. (N Mort Collection)

International Harvester was certainly one of them. It had a long and proud history of building trucks, heavy equipment, tractors, etc, as well as being one of the most important farm equipment manufacturers worldwide.

International's truck line prospered, and following WWII, along with its full line-up of large trucks, the company introduced a new line of pickup trucks, along with large station wagons and delivery/panel vans.

Half-way through 1957 a freshly restyled line of Travel-All wagons appeared and its new B-Series pickups shared the same styling.

In 1958 International also introduced an extended or double cab on its pickup truck line-up. Unique in its day, the four-door cab could accommodate six passengers, while still providing a full-size pickup bed.

Known for its Bonus-Load body, IH continued to offer its 'B' ½-ton pickup trucks, and in 1960 featured a cab with 25 percent more cargo space, and a rear box capable of hauling a load up to 8½-feet long. The wide-bodied cabs were also promoted as having easier ingress and egress, due to the fact there was no corner post protruding into the doorway.

The ½-ton B-Series was available in 110in, 114in, 126in, and 133in wheelbase versions. This beautifully restored two-tone white and blue 1960 B-100 is powered by the International 264ci Black Diamond Six. A gold and white anniversary model is in the background. (Courtesy Southland International)

The Model B-Series ½-ton pickup trucks were offered with a V8 engine as standard equipment and dubbed the V-266.

In 1960 International Harvester advertised in national magazines and boasted of its rugged, full line of trucks in a wide range of shapes and sizes. These advertisements often pictured its pickup trucks along with its heavy-duty tractors.

In 1961 International launched its new C-Series line of pickups that interestingly utilized the same B-Series cab and box, yet was cleverly restyled and sat lower into the frame for a totally different look.

As well as the new C-100 line-up International introduced its compact C-99 pickup truck in Canada. It was an attempt to compete directly with Studebaker's Lark-based Champ, while also stealing sales from the Big Three.

A black and white photograph was distributed to the Canadian press in February 1961, to help introduce the new 'Compact' C-99 ½-ton. The 152ci, slant 4-cylinder C-99 pickup was available only for the Canadian market. International described its Compact truck in its advertising as "…handles like the finest compact car!" (Courtesy Southland International)

Fresh styling and design resulted in the 1961 International ½-ton C-Series, being 5in lower (lowest in the industry), having a new torsion bar front suspension for a smoother ride, a stronger frame, longer wheelbase and an even roomier, more comfortable cab with "… one easy step and you're in." In reality it was the same B-Series cab and box cleverly reconfigured. (N Mort Collection)

This 1962 Canadian C-99 'Compact' ½-ton pickup truck is fully restored. All C-99s were built on a short 107in wheelbase. At the time it was the lowest priced ½-ton pickup truck on the Canadian market. After just two years the unique Canadian C-99 was dropped, only to reappear in the US as the 900. (Courtesy Southland International)

There was a strong family resemblance despite the C-99 being powered by a 4-cylinder engine and built on a shorter chassis. Most of the bodywork and components had been borrowed from the C-Series.

There were minimal changes made to the C-100 lineup for 1962, which from the outside appeared identical.

As well as a face-lift which included a new flat, egg crate-style grille and taller hood, in 1963 International changed the names of its pickups to C-1000 and C-900.

The C-Series continued on until 1964 with numerous improvements, such as improved steering, minor improvements in fittings under the hood, and a return to a chain attached tailgate. Strangely, the one handed tailgate was not reintroduced again until 1966.

For 1965 International introduced its new D-Series which consisted of another face-lift, interior, chassis and engine improvements, that the company felt was enough to rename its series. A better appointed 'Custom' cab was also added to the option list.

Another name change took place in 1966 with the introduction of a new A-Series that once again saw numerous minor improvements and another face-lift. Likewise, the same occurred in 1967 with the renamed B-Series line-up.

In 1968 the International 1000C was introduced. The familiar IH hood badge had disappeared. It could now be found on the front fender where the model designation had traditionally been affixed. The mesh grille was now black, as was the framing around the headlamp bezels. Side marker lights were one of the

The new-for-1967 1100B version sported a new, cleaner grille that combined fine mesh within a polished aluminum frame, and a center bar boldly spelling out 'International.' This was despite the fact that the familiar hefty black and red IH badge sat just above on the hood. Electric wipers replaced the old push-button type. (Courtesy Southland International)

Another change in the new B-Series in 1967 was a return to a shorter 8ft rather than 8½ft box. The change occurred sometime in 1967, as both sizes were originally listed in the specifications. A dual master cylinder and four-way flashers were two of the new legislated safety features. (Courtesy Southland International)

International had traditionally stressed its trucks were rugged, no-nonsense work vehicles, but in these changing times came the ad line, "Your wife drives it 50 miles to the hairdresser's and back. Is she a truck driver?" when referring to the latest International 1000C ½-ton. As a result of the changing market, the 1968 1000 was available with an optional Deluxe or Custom interior, seat covers, and Custom exterior trim for a much dressier look.
(N Mort Collection)

The all-new D-Series appeared in 1969, featuring flattened sides, a more angular, simplified grille, trim, and two-tone color. From 1969 to 1975 no substantial changes were made to the styling. This 1975 example is rare today; it was built in the shortened final year of production – the last light-duty International ½-ton pickup truck came off the assembly line on May 5, 1975. The smaller 4x4 Scout continued in production until 1980. (Courtesy Southland International)

numerous items added, due to the latest government mandated safety regulations.

As the decade came to a close, International finally introduced its D-Series, featuring all-new styling. The new pickups were styled after the more popular Scout. The 1000D and beefed-up 1100D ½-ton pickups were offered on a 115in or 131in wheelbase. The smaller 908C was left out of the line-up. Engine choices consisted of the standard 141hp, 240ci Six, or the optional 155hp, 266ci V8.

Despite its modern looks, the new line of pickups failed to spark sales, and would be dropped halfway through the 1970s.

Kaiser-Jeep Corporation was all about four-wheel-drive, but that didn't mean it was going to totally ignore the two-wheel-drive market. Although the emphasis remained on its go anywhere trucks, the 2WD version was offered for those who wanted a tough Jeep Gladiator pickup for in-town use and better fuel mileage. (N Mort Collection)

Kaiser-Jeep

There were 28 different Jeep models offered in 1960, and 31 in 1961 and 1962, yet average production remained at around 31,500 units a year.

A complete realignment of the company for 1963 saw a return to the lucrative 2WD pickup truck market, in an attempt to capture market share.

In 1963 a new 2WD Jeep Gladiator ½-ton pickup was unveiled, as part of the new Wagoneer and Gladiator line-up. The Jeep family resemblance was maintained through its vertically slotted tall front grille, albeit peaked in the center. An interesting feature was

the fact the lower body sills and underbody structural members were galvanized for increased longevity. The only engine offered was the 140hp, 230.5ci, OHC Hurricane six-cylinder. Sales increased, but by only 12,000 units with just a small percentage being 2WD ½-ton pickups.

Styling was basically unchanged in 1964, but a new lower compression, 130hp version of the Six was offered, and air-conditioning was also a new option.

1965 saw the Jeep nameplate changed to Kaiser-Jeep on all models, and two different Series being offered. The styling was virtually the same whether

All the new Gladiator pickup truck models were available in the smooth-sided Townside or traditional flared fender Thriftside in 2WD or 4WD. Optional equipment on both included independent front suspension, power brakes, power steering, and a four-speed or automatic transmission. (N Mort Collection)

The Jeep Gladiator Townside pickup truck models in 2WD were available in a 120in (J-200) or 126in (J-300) wheelbase, with four gross vehicle weights ranging from 4000 to 5600lb. This camper unit was optional on both the 2WD and 4WD Kaiser-Jeep pickups. (N Mort Collection)

"UNSTOPPABLE" 'JEEP' GLADIATOR

AVAILABLE IN 2 AND 4-WHEEL DRIVE

Few cosmetic changes were made to the exterior of the Jeep Gladiator pickup truck, other than in badging and some trim, as can be seen in this 1965 brochure. Although available in two-wheel-drive, the brochure stressed four-wheel-drive capabilities. Standard safety features were noted that by the end of the decade would be considered as very basic, such as seatbelts, a high-impact windscreen, an outside rearview mirror, a dual braking system, a padded dash, self-adjusting brakes, a padded sunvisor, four-way warning flashers, a windshield washer and dual speed wipers. (N Mort Collection)

you had a J-200 or a J-2000, but the GVW was increased. The biggest news was the availability of a 327ci V8.

While some of the Wagoneer models received a new hood and horizontal grille in 1966, the Gladiator pickup truck styling remained much the same as originally introduced.

In 1967 the model line-up shrunk, leaving only a basic Gladiator J-100 in the 2WD pickup truck models, and it, too, would disappear in 1968.

Despite the introduction of the Jeepster model, annual production remained at just over 38,000 units. As a result, American Motors Corporation (AMC) purchased Jeep from Kaiser Industries in February 1970, under whose management Jeep would begin to flourish.

THRIFTSIDE

As well as the Jeep Gladiator Townside pickup truck, a Thriftside rear-fendered version was offered. The all-steel box was rib reinforced, and the tops of the box sides were flanged and rolled for extra strength, as on this 1965 model. (N Mort Collection)

New approaches to the traditional ½-ton pickup trucks

Chevrolet Corvair 95

Despite decent sales in 1960, the Corvair, with its revolutionary design and style, was a flop compared to Ford's more conventional Falcon, that outsold it two to one at more than 435,000 units. The Corvair brochure stated this car "... doesn't need power steering, power brakes, a radiator, a water pump, anti-freeze, or even water."

Sales increased in 1961 with an expanded model line-up, but the bulk of the sales were due to the sporty appeal of the Monza version with its four-speed, all-synchromesh transmission.

A stylish, new 1961 Corvair 95 pickup was added in two versions – the more traditional Loadside and the extra-versatile Rampside. The Corvair 95 was available with a host of attractive options such as a chrome package, numerous driver comfort upgrades, two-tone paint, whitewall tires and full wheel discs.

The number '95' stemmed from the pickup trucks shorter 95in wheelbase. Power from its air-cooled, horizontally-opposed, four-cylinder engine was transferred via a standard 3-speed, optional 4-speed manual, or a Powerglide two-speed automatic.

The biggest flaw in this unique pickup concept was its uneven bed floor, which made loading difficult to the point where it was easier to drop things in from the side – truly a Loadside. Despite an optional plywood and angle iron section that provided a flat floor, this was an awkward addition to consistently install and remove.

The Loadside Corvair 95 was not a sales success, and a mere 2844 were built over a two-year period, while, the easier loading Rampside sold in promising numbers in 1961 with 10,787 being built.

The Corvair 95 pickups came in two models: the Loadside and the Rampside. The Loadside had a traditional rear tailgate, while the Rampside had the rear tailgate plus a handy side ramp. With its wide pickup box and a flat floor there was 80ft³ of cargo space. The deep, amidships storage well boosted the cargo space. Available at no extra cost was the optional three-section floor to provide a flat cargo box. (N Mort Collection)

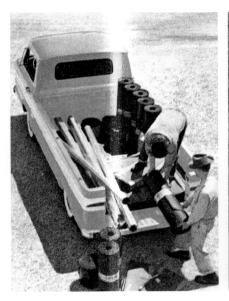

Far left: The overall length of a Corvair 95 pickup was 179¼in. It rode on a 95in wheelbase with a bed length of 103¼in with the tailgate up. When the tailgate was down there was an additional 15½in. It had a payload rating of 1900lb, which was 250lb more than an Econoline. The GVW was 4600lb.

Left: The side ramp on the Rampside was a novel idea that never caught on, even though it combined the economy of an air-cooled engine, the Corvair 95's relatively low price, and a hefty cargo capacity. The Rampside – with its unibody construction – couldn't withstand the rigorous daily toil, or eventual inherent rust.
(N Mort Collection)

Alas, that number fell to less than half in 1962, and basically half again in 1963.

By 1963 the Corvair 95 Loadside pickup truck was dropped from the line-up, while the Rampside continued, and was powered mid-year by a 102hp air-cooled engine.

Although Corvair production exceeded well over 200,000 units in 1963, that included just 2046 Rampside pickups. In 1964 only 851 Rampside pickups were built and so production was halted. In this final year a 164ci engine was available rated at 95hp or 110hp.

In 1965 with a new body style came a smaller Corvair range, that consisted of a convertible, and a two and four-door hardtop. There was no new pickup truck version considered.

Ford/Mercury Econoline

Ford introduced its new Econoline Van and Station Bus in 1961, and it seemed natural to also offer a pickup truck version. Despite its unit construction, the new Econoline ½-ton pickup had lots to offer. Visually identical to its higher volume sibling, the pickup truck offered an open cargo bed that was 89.5in long, 22.4in high and 63in wide.

The 'driver-forward' design was a COE (cab-over-engine), as the 86hp, 144ci six-cylinder motor sat between the driver and optional passenger's vinyl-covered seats. A 3-speed transmission was standard on this 90in wheelbase pickup. With an overall length of just 168.4in and width of 65in, the new Ford 'Falcon' Econoline pickup truck was ideal in crowded city streets and alleys, for deliveries and

Left: Ford's Econoline E-100 series were introduced in 1961, and in Canada there was a Mercury version. Ford saw its new Econolines as direct competition to the slightly smaller, but popular Transporter models from Volkswagen. Mercury pushed the new E-Series in Canada, and had special 'Owner's Reports' published almost immediately, hailing the attributes of the new Econoline van and pickup. In both Ford and Mercury guise, a Standard model, as well as a very basic Custom – in name if not execution – were offered. Right: Ford was not shy to point out the E100-series had the advantage of a "Flat floor (no rear engine hump) for easier loading," compared to its Corvair 95 rival. One company owner noted in its report that "Drivers also like its ease of handling and good visibility." Basic models had no exterior locks, no armrest, and a single sunvisor. Options included insulation, a padded dash top, and a glovebox door. (N Mort Collection)

service work. A total of 14,893 Econoline pickup buyers agreed.

For 1962 minimal detail changes were made to the parking lights and trim, but larger wheel bearings were fitted, and a 170ci Six was offered as an option. Surprisingly, sales slipped to 8140 units.

As well as its low loading deck, which was just 25in off the ground, the Econoline Pickup had a 48in-wide tailgate and a full 7ft of flat load length. Operators reported a saving of $100.00 a month in fuel, which was a very substantial sum when a gallon of gas sold for around 25 cents in Canada in 1961. (N Mort Collection)

In 1963 the styling of the Econoline ½-ton remained the same, but there were some changes, such as a heavy-duty 3-speed, fully synchronized transmission and amber-colored front turn signal lenses. More optional upgrades offered in mid-year include a column-shift, Dagenham-sourced, 4-speed transmission, a heavy-duty

package which include the bigger six, a tougher rear axle, stiffer springs, a reinforced frame and larger 14in wheels.

Sales bounced back slightly with 11,394 Standard and Custom Econolines being delivered.

Once again there were few changes in 1964 other than self-adjusting brakes and locking side vent

For 1962 the Econoline Pickup was promoted for what it was named after – economy. There were few luxuries, and even the heater, radio, and passenger seat were extras. Ford saw substantial savings for operators in gas, oil, tires, replacement parts and license fees – in some areas. The longer 7ft box was rated higher than most ½-tons – even up to ¾-tons, according to Ford. (N Mort Collection)

windows. Two new options were an alternator rather than generator, and an automatic transmission.

Sales in 1964 tumbled to just 5184 pickups.

There were, finally, some major changes made to the E-100 pickups in 1965. There were two new six-cylinder engines offered. The aging 144ci engine was

Just as Chevrolet and Dodge discovered, the new forward cab-style Ford and Mercury designs were not the big sellers that were hoped for when the decade began. Introduced in 1961 these Econoline pickups would disappear early in 1967. The van version carried on until 1968, when it was replaced by a completely redesigned model. Very few changes took place in either styling or engineering over the years, and a new pickup version in the E-Series was not offered in 1968. (N Mort Collection)

dropped, and in its place came a 200ci and a 240ci Six.

With the additional power, the engines were mounted on a tubular crossmember rather than the previous cantilever arms. Heftier bumpers were fitted and the seating and heating improved.

A gauge package was optional which replaced the oil and alternator warning lights. An alternator was made standard.

A Deluxe pickup was offered only in Poppy Red with added trim and chrome bumpers.

Whereas sales in 1965 increased slightly to 7405 pickup trucks, in comparison the Econoline van models were approaching 70,000 units and climbing.

Few changes occurred in 1966 other than emergency flashers becoming standard equipment, as did the padded dash and a locking glovebox door later that year.

Some changes were made in '67 due to government regulations, such as a dual braking system with a failure warning light. Other new standard equipment included two-speed wipers and never before offered, back-up lights. Production fell from the 1966 meagre total of 3090 units to just 2015. The 1967 Econoline pickups would be sold into 1968, although still designated as '67 models. The

For 1964 Dodge introduced its Cab-Forward A100 vans and pickup trucks, but these didn't appear in showrooms until May or June of that year. This new 'Compact' pickup truck, with its engine between the two bucket seats, was powered by a 101hp, 140ci Slant Six engine, with a larger Slant Six being optional. A more powerful engine would be added in 1965 in the form of the 174hp, 273ci V8. A 3-speed column-mounted annual transmission was standard equipment. Despite great optimism, production totaled just 11,046 units. (N Mort Collection)

total production over the seven years was just 52,121 of the E100 pickups, compared to 492,212 Econoline vans.

Dodge/Fargo A100

In 1964 Dodge built a COE design that was marketed first as purely a utilitarian pickup, but ended up being rather more performance-oriented by the time production was halted in 1968.

The stylish A100 was introduced to compete with Ford's compact Econoline pickup trucks. Both of these vehicles may have looked somewhat like Volkswagen's bus-based pickup, but these RWD trucks were true COE, rather than having the engine in the rear like the VW and Chevy's failed Corvair 95 Rampside and Loadside.

The Ford Econoline may have outsold the A100, but because of the A100's drag racing heritage and the Chrysler muscle car performance image during the sixties, today the A100 has a greater collector demand.

Despite the engine between the two standard bucket seats, the A100 had a generous, but very functional interior with its rubber mats, painted metal and fiberglass panels, as can be seen in this 1966 A100. Sitting in an A100 was a bit like driving a small bus. Back then its seating position was quite different, but with today's FWD minivans, most driver's would find it second nature. (N Mort Collection)

Even after offering V8 power as an option to the standard Slant Six, sluggish sales of the A100 Dodge pickups failed to increase. In 1966 a mere 235 V8 versions were built of these stylish-looking ½-tons. A painted front bumper was standard. (N Mort Collection)

In 1964 the compact A100 pickup was one of just three models based on this design. Like Ford, Dodge offered a van and a multi-passenger Sportsman wagon. The load-level floor of the A100 made the loading and delivery of items easy.

The A100s were shorter, wider and taller than either the Ford Econoline, or Chevy Corvair 95. At 2790lb it weighed about as much as the Chevy, but was 200lb heavier than the Econoline. The pickup bed measured 213ft³, and the A100 had a GVW rating of 5200lb. The spare tire mounted on the inside of the box was unique among the three.

Powerwise there were two economical engines available; the 101bhp, 170ci and the 140bhp, 225ci, which were both slant sixes. The 225ci Six was actually the biggest engine in the compact truck field. A 3-speed manual was standard, while the 3-speed LoadFlite automatic mounted on the dash was optional.

At the 1965 Chicago Auto Show, an A100 Camper Wagon was unveiled, but otherwise the A100 compact trucks looked virtually the same, and would throughout its production life, except for minor trim changes.

The big news was the availability of the 174hp,

Opposite: Built on a 90in wheelbase, the A100 had a generous 7ft box with its tailgate up. Payload allowances ranged from 920lb up to 2160lb, and this 1966 version offered 14 or 15in wheels. The base Slant Six engine produced only 101hp, but the top-of-the-line V8 was rated at over twice that, at 210hp. (N Mort Collection)

The interior of the Dodge A100 pickups was inviting, but not luxurious. Ingress and egress was easy with its large, wide-opening doors. The split-windscreen was not seen as a throwback to an earlier era, but the heat and noise from the engine were. (N Mort Collection)

273ci V8. This was the first step in providing buyers the option of turning their A100 into something more than a utilitarian workhorse. It was also the first year of Dodge's five year/50,000 mile warranty that caught the entire truck industry off guard.

Built with the only V8 in its class, and appropriately fitted with stronger axles, heavy-duty suspension and larger wheels and tires, the A100 was becoming a great dual-purpose work and play vehicle. Production increased in 1965 to 22,348 units.

In 1966, the A100 continued with only minor changes and production rose slightly to 23,363 pickups.

An even larger V8 was introduced in 1967 for the A100, replacing the 273ci engine with an optional 210hp, 318ci motor.

Safety regulations resulted in standard padded instrument panel, padded dual sunvisors, and a dual braking system.

A slightly different look came in the form of optional rear quarter windows as part of a custom cab package, or could be ordered separately. Other optional niceties inside included a cigar lighter, a driver's armrest, a chrome horn ring, and more interior sound and heat insulation. Bright-finish hub caps were also available. An extended 108in wheelbase was offered on the van and Sportsman models only.

1968 saw more luxurious interior appointments including color-keyed interiors, while outside there was a new grille, and two-tone paint schemes were offered.

The last full year of production continued to see only mild upgrades, which included a fully-synchronized 3-speed manual transmission that became available for the V8. The 190ci Slant Six replaced the old 170ci engine.

In April, 1970 the A100 was replaced by the 1971 B-Series vans, but no pickup was offered.

Drag racer Bill 'Maverick' Golden drove a 426 Hemi-powered A100, while the legendary 'Little Red Wagon' was built by Dick Branstner, Roger Lindamood and the Dodge Truck engineers, as a colorful exhibition machine.

The 'Little Red Wagon' featured a special subframe which held the Hemi engine and rear-mounted TorqueFlite transmission, 10in slicks and a dragster fuel tank. Photographs of the pickup always pictured it doing 'wheelies' as it came off the line due to its power and short 90in wheelbase. The impressive 'Little Red Wagon' was capable of a 10-second, ¼-mile time that was slowed by a parachute affixed to the tailgate.

As a result the A100s which are restored are usually not stock, as most came with six-cylinder engines. Since Chrysler offered them with V8s and all the Mopar accessories available, it's no wonder these trucks are popular as alternative muscle vehicles.

In its last full year of production, the 1969 A100 was difficult to distinguish from the original 1964 version. Two-toning helped, but just like its big cousins of COE design, the positive attributes of maneuverability and overall size were not enough to overcome the noise, heat and servicing problems.
(N Mort Collection)

Chevrolet El Camino

Introduced in 1959 the Chevrolet El Camino would eventually fill a shrinking niche market up until 1987, but easily outlast its Ford Ranchero rival.

When it debuted, the El Camino – Spanish for 'the road' – was the flagship of the Chevy light-duty truck line. It was built in response to Ford's Ranchero car/pickup that had been such a sales success when it appeared in 1957. A total of 22,246 El Caminos were built in 1959.

Yet, the 1960 El Camino was downright sober in appearance and performance, compared to the previous

The 1960 Chevrolet El Camino strongly resembled the rest of the restyled 1959 full-size Chevrolet car models. Once again it was based on the two-door station wagon platform, as Chevrolet had simply removed the wagon roof from the front seatback of its large Biscayne and dropped in a pickup truck box. Sales plummeted to only 14,163 units, as Ford's new compact Falcon-based Ranchero stole the limelight. Note, since the late 1930s it was common practice to distort drawings and photographs to make a car or truck appear longer, lower, and wider and thus convey a sportier, faster vehicle, as seen in this El Camino brochure.

For 1960, economy was pushed on the new low-priced El Camino. The price dropped US$340, and the utilitarianism of the El Camino was the focus of its ad campaign. A fuel-saving 170hp, 283ci Turbo-Fire V8 was offered on this now up to 4900lb GVW pickup, or you could go for all-out performance with a 335hp eight-cylinder. The pickup box had a loadspace of up to 32½ft³ being 72¼ft long, 64¼ft wide and 12⅞in deep. (N Mort Collection)

year. Cosmetically, the reason for the rear end being toned down, was the fact Ford's more conservative styling had proven to be more popular with buyers.

As a result, for 1960 the El Camino was restyled with flatter wings, a conservative horizontal bar grille, and far less curves; also no big block V8 engine was offered. The once flagship was now the lowest-priced, full-size Chevrolet available, at US$2400, and sales declined dramatically.

For 1961 the El Camino was dropped from the line-up, as Chevy's rear-engine Corvair compact could not be easily converted into a Ford Falcon-like competitor.

In 1965 a 300hp, 327 V8 could be ordered, and the horsepower grew steadily. The following year a 325hp and 350hp Turbo-Jet 396 V8 was offered. These ½-ton American pickups were aimed at specific markets other than the traditional truck market. For example, as a car-truck, the El Camino also provided muscle car performance at lower pickup truck insurance rates.

(Andrew Mort)

This 1965 El Camino interior could have been mistaken for a hot Chevelle's front cockpit. Behind the seat was a big enough space to house the spare tire, as well as an air valve to the rear shocks for boosting load capacity. (Andrew Mort)

Then, in 1964, the El Camino name and concept was resurrected, but this time as a pickup, based on the mid-size Chevelle car line. This was a two-door station wagon that was easy to convert. Horsepower was selling cars, and Chevrolet would offer this new El Camino with lots of engine options from two six-cylinders to three V8s. Most powerful was the 250hp, 327ci V8. Standard and Custom versions were offered.

The new Chevelle, despite its shorter 201½in overall length and 115in wheelbase, actually lent itself to a bigger loadspace than the original full-size-based models.

In 1965, apart from minor front end restyling, the big changes were under the hood, with increases in horsepower. In 1966, however, buyers had the amazing choice of 24 different engine and transmission choices.

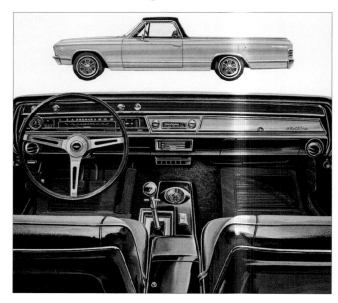

Chevrolet was at the forefront of performance sports models with its Corvair, Camaro, Chevelle and Impala SS models. The formula in the sixties was easy: a powerful V8 engine, a tachometer on the dash, a walnut grained steering wheel, bucket seats, posi-traction, mag-style wheel covers, a vinyl roof, and a console with a gearshift – the El Camino had it all in '67 and much more. (N Mort Collection)

In 1967 Chevrolet asked you to "Cast your eye on this collector's item." They didn't mean the Stutz Bearcat on the trailer either. The El Camino came with 60 powertrain combinations. You could order from two Sixes and five V8 engines up to 350 horses, and you could match your engine to one of five manual or two automatic transmissions. Of the two automatic transmissions the 2-speed Powerglide was a very poor second to the much better 3-speed Turbo Hydra-Matic. Multiple rear axle ratios were also offered. (N Mort Collection)

During the 1960s there were many performance-oriented versions of the Chevrolet El Camino, that provided tire-burning muscle car power and acceleration, along with its inherent hauling capabilities. In 1969 the biggest engine offered was the 350hp version of the 396ci V8. The production life story of the El Camino – and its later 1971-onwards GMC brethren, the Sprint and Caballero – included a multitude of ever-changing, very different sibling models. The development of each subsequent model generation included changes in platform sizes and model line-ups. (N Mort Collection)

The 396ci versions went on to create a long-lasting image with enthusiasts.

The '66 El Camino could also be ordered with even more luxury options. The Custom models featured deep-pile carpeting, upgraded upholstery, bucket seats, a console and A/C.

Despite being the last year for the second generation El Camino, the 1967 version was extensively restyled. There was a new grille, front and rear bumpers, front fenders and hood, heavier-looking trim moldings, plus some trendy wrap-around tail lamps. Still, the El Camino retained the same 78½in-long box as the '64 model.

In 1968 a completely redesigned El Camino 396 SS was introduced, finally, featuring all the SS goodies.

A minor face-lift occurred in 1969, and the SS 396 option package offered on the Custom El Camino included a dressed 325hp, Turbo-Jet 396 engine, front power disc brakes, a three-speed floorshift, dual exhausts, a matte black grille and special hood, a heavy-duty suspension, a trim and badging package, and 14x7in wheels with redline tires. Optional aluminum head 350 and 375hp versions were offered, and total sales reached 48,385 units of these 'flying buttress' roof models.

The El Camino underwent a further face-lift in 1970 in keeping with the Chevelle. As well as the 396, the Custom version could be ordered with a 360hp, or LS6 450hp V8. The LS6 El Camino was capable of 13 second quarter miles at over 108mph. The El Camino was now very high in muscle car power league.

It should be noted that, at the end of 1979, Ford decided to halt production of its rival Ranchero model, which left this niche pickup market solely to the Chevy El Camino and its GMC counterpart the Sprint, which was later renamed Caballero.

Despite this, in 1980 El Camino sales dropped from 58,008 units to 40,932, while the GMC version dropped from 6952 to just 4742 units. These build numbers continued to slide until 1983 when production increased slightly by around 1300 units and reached a marginally better high of 24,010 versions of the El Camino.

In 1984 production slipped again to 22,997 units and that downward trend then continued to the end. In the El Camino's final year in 1987 fewer than 14,000 examples of these special ½-ton pickups were built. And, despite the fact production ceased in July 1987, some 420 El Caminos were actually sold and titled as 1988 models. It should also be pointed out that production was moved to a General Motors' plant in Mexico in 1985.

Ford Ranchero

Ford's Ranchero was the industry's first car-based pickup when introduced in 1957. Chevrolet rushed to compete and introduced its rival El Camino in 1959. Both were based on their respective full-size car lines, but in 1960 Ford dropped the full-size Ranchero, while Chevrolet struggled on with a restyled El Camino.

Instead, Ford reintroduced a smaller Ranchero, based on its all-new 'Compact' Falcon, in the late fall of 1959. The Ranchero became known as the Falcon Ranchero, and despite its overall shorter dimensions it was still a capable ½-ton pickup truck, as well as being declared 'America's Lowest Priced Pickup.' This was an even greater change in concept when you consider the Ranchero had been America's most luxurious pickup in 1959.

The Falcon-based Ranchero had a 109.5in wheelbase compared to the old 118in-long model. The overall length had shrunk from 208in to 189in. The base engine was now the 90hp, 144ci OHV, six-cylinder,

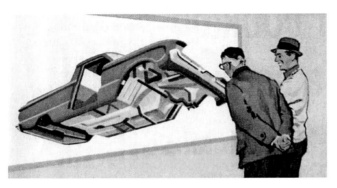

The new, compact-sized 1960 Ford Ranchero ½-ton pickup was not only the lowest priced on the market, but was able to get 30mpg on a tank of 'regular' low octane gasoline. Like the Falcon model cars it was a unibody design with bolt-on front fenders. Chassis-wise the new Ranchero featured an independent front suspension, variable-rate rear leaf springs, and dual-servo hydraulic brakes. There was 31.6ft³ of load space in the 6ft box, as well as 42in of flat floor between the inner wheelhousings. The Ranchero's 800lb payload outshone the big El Camino with its 700lb limit. (N Mort Collection)

The Ranchero continued to utilize all of the compact Falcon model's styling, bumpers and trim in 1961. Improvements on Ford's Ranchero saw a lower spring rate, new A-arm bushings, an anti-rust rocker, and underbody zinc treatment added. Inside, the dome light was moved to the roof, and the spare tire was mounted behind the seat for 'easy roll-out.' Easier maintenance was noted due to bolt-on fenders. Production totaled 20,937 Ranchero pickups, down from the 1960 recorded 21,027 units. Still, overall, Ford marketing was satisfied with the model's success. (N Mort Collection)

compared to the 1959's 223ci six. A 170ci six would later become optional on the Falcon Ranchero. No longer could you order your Ranchero with a V8. The only other powertrain option was the Fordomatic transmission instead of a standard 3-speed manual. Two-toning was offered, with just the roof top being a contrasting color.

Although half a decade before the Mustang and Bronco, Ford was already pushing the western theme in its brown vinyl seats and trim with steer head embossing which would continue throughout the Falcon Ranchero model's lifetime.

In 1960 the Deluxe interior featured a black and white or red and white vinyl, with white steering wheel.

For 1961 a more intricate, convex grille was the only real cosmetic change on the Falcon Ranchero. A Deluxe Trim Package was again offered, as well as a revised and much more distinctive two-toning paint combination that included the A and B-pillars, resulting in a very dressy-looking Ranchero, especially with the chrome fender ornaments.

Numerous suspension improvements were made to improve the ride and handling in 1961.

In 1962 for the first time the Falcon Ranchero received a real face-lift with a new bumper that included integrated parking lights. There was a flatter, chrome-trimmed new hood design, that was less 'power bulge' and more 'scoop,' and a revised grille. The taillights were also modified, but still round.

Also introduced was a Deluxe interior and exterior package, a Safety package, and a list of individual upgrade options made available.

Very minor grille and tail lamps changes were made in 1963, but self-adjusting brakes, an aluminized tailpipe, and electric windshield wipers were added. The six-cylinder engine now had hydraulic valve-lifters, the 3-speed transmission was made fully-synchronized, and a larger front stabilizer bar was fitted.

The Ranchero underwent a metamorphosis in 1964. Still based on the Falcon, it was fully restyled as Ford was moving from its very rounded shapes on its car lines to a trimmer, more angular and sculpted

New Falcon Ranchero—America's smartest pickup! Gives you all the flair and fashion of a Falcon car . . . all its riding comfort and handling ease! Famous Falcon economy, too! Choice of two gas-saving engines. 800 lbs. load capacity!

Introduced in 1960, other than a slightly changed grille and some trim, the 1962 version remained virtually identical. Ford advertised its compact-sized, Falcon-based Ranchero as "America's smartest pickup! Gives you all the flair and fashion of a Falcon car . . . " Other less obvious, but more important improvements were an aluminized muffler, a fuel filter, increased brake lining areas, upgraded carburettor and choke controls, and an optional clutch interlock. For 1962, the Ranchero still only boasted a choice of two engines for its 800lb load capacity. (N Mort Collection)

In its last year with the first generation Falcon styling, a new horizontal grille design and chrome trim on the crown of front fenders allowed for instant 1963 recognition. Mid-year there was the introduction of new V6 and V8 options with a 4-speed transmission. The growl of the new 164hp, 260ci V8, introduced mid-year, was what caught most people's attention. It was the start of the new sporty, high performance Falcons, that would change the compact line's image considerably – including the Ranchero. Production decreased to 18,533 units, despite Ford's overall increase in truck sales. (N Mort Collection)

form. It was a ½in longer and lower, but the wheelbase remained 109.5in.

The rear bed was reconfigured and made an inch lower, which resulted in a drop in loadspace to 30ft³. New interiors were offered with unique Deluxe features and vinyl patterns and colors.

An improved maintenance schedule increased the routine 6000 mile maintenance to 36,000 miles on major chassis lubrication, coolant, fuel and air filter changes. The '64 Ranchero also came with a 24,000 mile or 24-month full powertrain warranty.

Despite these positive changes, sales in 1964 only reached a disappointing 9916 units in the Standard model 66A; 1135 in the Deluxe 66B version; and another 235 Deluxe Ranchero 66H models that came equipped with bucket seats.

The 1965 Falcon Ranchero continued to sport its leaner, more angular, styling with minimal cosmetic changes. The 260ci V8 was replaced with a smoother 200hp or 225hp 289ci, to help compete with the new El Camino which had

The more angular, restyled for 1964, Falcon Ranchero also featured an integral cab and pickup box, and was promoted as being an all-welded in heavy-gauge steel, single-unit, body-frame construction designed for maximum strength. The cab-wide back windscreen provided excellent rearward vision. The 6ft pickup box provided 31½ft³ of load space, and the new tailgate featured a single latch handle for one-handed operation. The 1964 rear end styling was unique to the Falcon Ranchero, sedan delivery and station wagon. The big news for '64 though was the continued availability of the 164hp, 260ci V8, as well as three six-cylinder choices and a 4-speed transmission. (N Mort Collection)

appeared in 1964. As well as offering four-on-the-floor, there was a new 3-speed automatic. Sales remained steady with 10,539 Standard and 7734 Deluxe Rancheros sold.

In 1966 a very new looking Falcon Ranchero debuted, with plenty of the larger Fairlane overtones. New Texas Longhorn steer head emblems were placed on the B-pillars and rear tailgate. The Standard Ranchero was well appointed, with the Custom adding color-keyed carpeting, a deluxe instrument and door panel, grained

vinyl in a unique two-tone pleated pattern with bucket seats, and a floor shift being optional. Buyers responded and production increased to 21,760 units in 1966.

In 1967, in order to even more directly compete with the intermediate Chevelle-based El Camino, Ford abandoned the remnants of its compact Falcon-based Ranchero, and responded with an all-new Fairlane version.

The North American automakers had discovered

Once again, the Ranchero grille was changed to provide a fresh look for '66. While the front end styling followed its Falcon heritage, the long hood hinted at shorter deck, with a slight Coke bottle shape was very much in the popular Mustang mode. In its last year based on the Ford Falcon, the 1966 Ranchero, like the entire Falcon line-up, was already sharing many components found on the Fairlane – even its larger platform. The next year's model would be based entirely on the new intermediate-sized, luxury-oriented Ranchero. (N Mort Collection)

For 1966 the Ranchero featured a larger 39.1ft³ load space in its rear bed, and a carrying capacity of up to 1250lb. The maximum GVW was 4410lb. The wheelbase had been increased to 113in and the front and rear track to 58in. Total length was up to 198.8in, and an overall width of 74in. Likewise, inside was roomier and the side glass was now curved. The tailgate was a strong selling point on the Ranchero, with its one-handed latch system that continued into production through 1979. (N Mort Collection)

While the standard American pickup truck was now a common sight in American middle class driveways and garages, the '66 Ranchero was even more the gentleman farmer's pickup, as well as being portrayed at home in far more exclusive settings in 1966, despite its hauling capabilities. There was a Ranchero for those who were practical, one for buyers who wanted luxury, and yet another who were more performance oriented. More safety features were also added, such as seatbelts, a padded dash and visor pad to shade the instruments, an emergency light flasher unit and a rearview mirror as standard. (N Mort Collection)

An 'Intermediate' was the industry's catch-word for a car larger than a 'Compact,' but smaller than a 'Full-Size' model. 1967 brought an all-new, fully 'intermediate-sized' Fairlane-based Ranchero. How often the Ranchero actually hauled a full load, and the effect on performance, was rarely tested in period publications. An unloaded 270hp, 390ci V8 Ranchero was capable of 0-60mph in 9.4 seconds, with a ¼-mile time of 17 seconds and 80mph. With its bed empty the heavy front end, versus the light rear, resulted in considerable oversteer and ploughing. Thus, handling was more like the average pickup, than the usual high-performance car. (N Mort Collection)

that not everyone wanted a smaller compact car, while many buyers, young and older, who usually only had an occasional third passenger, or a dog, didn't need to drive around in a full-size car.

Ford's new 'Intermediate' Fairlane Ranchero was well received by the press and the public. In the vernacular of the 1960s, enthusiasts felt the new Ranchero styling was 'beauty' and, with an optional 390ci V8, it was very 'cool.'

Although handling wasn't praised, it was fast, sporty and fun to drive in most situations. Cruising with a powerful V8 in a sporty-looking car or pickup, with relatively inexpensive gas, was a very enjoyable experience in North America in the 1960s.

The testers in *Motor Trend* (6/67) noted that they particularly enjoyed the new Ranchero, but were mystified by why they would never consider buying one.

"We compared notes with other staff members who had time in the Ranchero and all of us had the same reaction: none of us would want to have one or could use one as our only car. Even as a second car, there were other body styles more useful to us. Despite these considerations, all of us liked the Ranchero, and to a man, wished there were some way we could have one."

The writers went on to say, "This is a pretty emotional response to a vehicle with a practical purpose, but the looks we got from other motorists were pure admiration, and had nothing to do with how much top soil it could carry."

The quad-stacked headlamps and grille proved the new Ranchero was from the Fairlane family. Three models were offered: the Fairlane, the Fairlane 500, and the Fairlane 500XL Ranchero. The 500XL version bore a medallion on the front grille, plus it came with bucket seats and a center console, and special trim. The 225hp,

BEST IDEA YET IN PICKUP LUXURY! ALL-NEW RANCHERO BY FORD

Luxury, as well as performance, was stressed in 1968. The top-of-the-line 500XL had been renamed the Ranchero GT, which came with a unique side striping package, and lots of GT badges. The Ranchero GT came equipped with the 325hp, 390ci V8, and was praised for its low, comfortable, very Ford Torino-like ride. The Ranchero GT got the stylish, as well as comfortable, Torino interior that had been designed to cut fatigue, and allowed plenty of leg and elbow room. Only the horseshoe-type handle on the gearshift was criticized by the press as being awkward. Two other models were also offered. (N Mort Collection)

ALL-NEW RANCHERO BY FORD

Despite being new in 1967, Ford promoted its 1968 Ranchero as being "all-over new." Like its El Camino competition, the 1968 Ranchero was moving upmarket, with its overall larger size. Its quad lighting was now horizontal in its new grille, and the taillights were changed. The vent windows were eliminated. Mechanical changes consisted of a new control arm in the front suspension, and other minor upgrades. (N Mort Collection)

289ci V8 was discontinued in mid-year. An energy-absorbing steering wheel was the latest standard safety feature.

For 1968 only minor cosmetic and mechanical changes were made, but the top-of-the-line Fairlane was now dubbed the Torino.

As the decade ended Ford's Ranchero changed little other than receiving a dramatic new hood scoop and a slightly revised grille. Numerous other minor changes were made inside and out, but the biggest news was the offering of the optional 428 engine package.

Ford was promoting its Ranchero in 1969 as more car than truck. "Fine-car luxury in a hard-working pickup. It looks just like a fine car. Rides and handles like one. Colour-coordinated interiors with choice of bucket seats, AM/FM stereo radio, SelectAire conditioner, power steering and power front disc brakes." (N Mort Collection)

By 1969 the horsepower race was in full swing, and the most powerful V8s were being dropped into anything that might sell. The Ranchero was no exception. With its luxury appointments you could order Ford's ultimate V8, the 428 Cobra Jet Ram Air V8. The package included a performance and handling package, a larger radiator, battery, and a special induction system via the functional hood scoop. Cast aluminum valve covers, and other chrome dress-up features made the 428 look even more impressive when the hood was lifted. (N Mort Collection)

Popular pickup close-ups

1961 Chevrolet Corvair 95 Rampside

The Corvair was unique in the entire General Motors line-up with its new Fisher 'Monostrut' body.

The 1960 Corvair was Chevrolet's answer to the Volkswagen, rather than to AMC's Rambler, Studebaker's Lark, Ford's new Falcon and Chrysler's Plymouth Valiant/Dodge Dart.

Chevy even went so far as to adopt the rear-mounted, air-cooled engine layout that Volkswagen had so successfully developed and marketed.

The 108in wheelbase Corvair was originally powered by a four-main bearing, 139.6ci flat-six engine fitted with twin, single-barrel Rochester carbs.

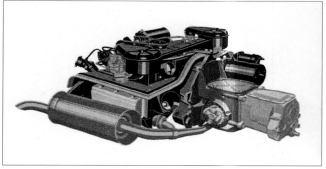

Chevrolet bragged about its new air-cooled powerplant design. "It's the most dramatic automotive development in decades, combining a totally new engine and transaxle drive unit into a remarkable compact, lightweight power package!" The '95' had an 80hp, 145ci, air-cooled six-cylinder engine when introduced, but grew in cubic inches and horsepower over the next few years. The side vents above the rear wheelwells were the first clue this truck was a rear-engine pickup. (N Mort Collection)

Although the Corvair 95 looked like a COE design, its air-cooled engine sat in the rear, following its sibling namesake car line-up. The ½-ton pickup's overall design featured styling cues seen on the car line-up, to tie-in the family resemblance, but still retained a distinctive look with its additional chrome and unique front grille. Total Loadside production was just 2844 units, whereas the initially more popular Rampside had a final production number of 17,786 trucks. (N Mort Collection)

The Corvair 95 Rampside featured a heavy-duty cargo ramp that swung down flush with a deep well at the side of the cargo box. The 4ft-wide opening allowed heavy equipment and freight to be loaded without lifting, or hand trucks and wheeled equipment to be easily rolled onboard. The loading floor was less than 14in off the ground, which was 10in less than Ford's Econoline pickup. When closed, the ramp was flush with the side of the box, and was secured by double-spring locks, as well as a safety catch. The top edge of the ramp door was padded to help avoid damage when loading. (N Mort Collection)

As well as hauling convenience and capabilities, Chevrolet also promoted the Corvair 95 Rampside on its cab comfort. The roomy interior featured a full-width flat floor with the absence of engine heat and noise. Big door openings, a deep-cushioned, full-width bench seat and plenty of options, such as a right-hand sunshade, left-hand armrest, cigarette lighter and bright instrument panel trim, provided a pleasant driving environment. (N Mort Collection)

It was lower than the other domestic compact competition, an average of 1300lb lighter, and about 2½ft shorter with a length of 180in. The fact it had a flat floor with no driveshaft bulge helped the public relations people brag it could carry six in comfort.

The Corvair was also the only compact American model offered with independent suspension on all four wheels. It was heralded by car enthusiast magazines

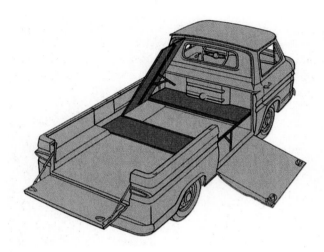

A popular option on the Rampside was the easily fitted and removed level-load floor which covered the nearly 28in well to provide a flat floor in the entire rear box. When in place the cover created a sizable storage compartment that was secured when the ramp door was closed. (N Mort Collection)

when introduced, and won the prestigious *Motor Trend* magazine 'Car of the Year' award.

A full range of Corvair models were ultimately introduced that included four-door sedan models, a coupe – the performance, upmarket version Monza coming in mid-year, a convertible known as the Spyder in 1962, a van, a station wagon, and the ½-ton pickup truck versions designated as the Corvair 95 models.

The all-new for 1961 Corvair 95 cab-forward pickup truck was available in two versions. The novel, side-loading Rampside and slightly more traditional Loadside.

As collector vehicles, these Corvair ½-ton pickups are very rare. Either worked to death, or victims of rust in snowy areas with lots of road salt, resulted in very few surviving. At the same time, like the Corvair car line, the Corvair 95 pickup truck has only a small, dedicated collector following, and thus, an equivalent condition traditional ½-ton Chevrolet commands equal or usually more in the marketplace.

In 1966 the Chevrolet C10 would be left basically the same, other than minor upgrades in safety equipment and drivetrain changes that were made throughout the various GM Divisions. An optional 'Custom Appearance Package' included added windscreen and roof pillar brightwork, a silver anodized front grille, additional steering wheel and dashboard chrome, and two-tone interior door panels. (Andrew Mort)

1966 Chevrolet C10

By 1966 the Chevrolet C10 was a familiar sight on the roads and around towns in North America. When introduced in 1960 these ½-ton pickup trucks were like a breath of fresh air with an all-new cab, new frame and re-engineered suspension. The C-series were just rounded enough to avoid being too boxy with its sculptured sides, low stance and overall trim, fit looks.

Inside the cab for '66 were two sets of seatbelts, and air-conditioning could be ordered as an in-dash option. Other items available included a heavy-duty electrical system, power steering, power brakes, and a tachometer. (Andrew Mort)

One of the few changes made by the factory in '66 was the move to rectangular side badges, complete with the Chevy bow-tie. This 1966, teal blue and white Chevrolet C10 shortbox was left with a 'preservation' finish of a well-worn teal color paint, and featured aged So-Cal signage on the door, along with other numerous graphics. The white-painted bumpers and trim were also treated to this attractive patina. New vintage, freshly-painted steel wheels were shod in wide whitewall radials, with new, shiny chrome hub caps and trim rings added. (Andrew Mort)

Although saddled, by 1966, with some aging styling nuances in its final year of production, the C10's overall design had held-up well. Seatbelts, dual mirrors, two-speed windscreen wipers, and backup lights were made standard to help sales.

Exterior changes for 1966 were virtually nil, other than some new paint colors. Inside, the seat upholstery vinyl materials were different, and came in a wider range of colors.

Engine choices included a standard 155hp, 250ci Six, or an optional 170hp, 292ci Six; the 283ci V8, and the 220hp, 327ci V8 in mid-year. The standard transmission was the 3-speed on the column, with optional transmissions being the 3-speed with overdrive, a 3-speed wide-ratio, a 4-speed, and the 2-speed Powerglide automatic. The C10 had a GVW of 5000lb.

Standard under the hood for '66 was a more powerful 150hp, 250ci Six, but there was the optional 220hp, 327ci V8 engine as an option. (Andrew Mort)

For 1966 the Chevrolet C10 ½-ton pickup truck was available as either a Stepside or Fleetside and both were offered with either a 6½ or 7½ft box. Production totaled over 300,000 units with the longer 127in wheelbase outselling the shorter 115in wheelbase by around 50,000 units. The C10 Fleetside ½-ton was once again Chevrolet's best-selling truck in the 366 model line-up.

1968 Dodge Adventurer

Replacing the 'Custom Sports Special' was the all-new for 1968 Dodge 'Adventurer,' which was promoted as a work truck, as well as a sports truck. Standard work truck features included Dodge's Cushion Beam Suspension, 140hp, 225 Slant Six, an oil filter, 37-amp alternator, a 3-speed column-mounted, synchro-shift transmission, a self-adjusting, dual braking system with

In the 'Swinging Sixties' pretty girls with long, usually blonde hair, miniskirts, and sultry or pouty looks, were used to help sell cars and trucks. And, while some women were burning their bras in protest, others were dropping them to help further their careers or express their new found freedom. The sex taboos of generations were disappearing quickly. Advertising companies knew sex sold, and automakers around the world took advantage of this. Dodge's sales brochures were filled with pretty girls, so no one was shocked in 1968 to see a girl posed on the hood of a pickup truck – even one called 'Adventurer.' (N Mort Collection)

Introducing Dodge

The 'Adventurer' nameplate appeared in 1968. It was promoted as a dual-purpose pickup truck designed for work and play. It proved to be very popular, and the model carried on into the next decade. (N Mort Collection)

warning light, Oriflow shock absorbers, turn signals, backup lights, a traffic hazard warning system, push-button door locks, a custom fresh air heater/defroster, a padded instrument panel, padded dual sunvisors, dual armrests, a driver adjustable handbrake, high-level ventilation, variable-speed wipers, windscreen washers, a jack and wheel wrench.

Standard Comfort items consisted of a 6-way adjustable seat, a choice of four color-keyed interiors, carpeting, fiberglass door trim panels, additional insulation against sound and weather, and glare reducing trim.

As well as the standard interior, you could order bucket seats with a padded storage console/folding armrest that could double for a third seat.

Outside there was plenty of eye-catching brightwork and the usual array of badges.

There were two power options for those constantly hauling heavy loads or wanting a little more 'sport.' V8-power came in two sizes. The 318ci was rated at 210hp, while you could go for more with the 258hp, 383ci engine. Two optional transmissions were offered in the form of the dash-mounted 3-speed automatic, or a fully-synchro, heavy-duty 4-on-the-floor.

The Dodge Adventurer trucks were described as being "... designed to lead a double life." The brochures stressed "You might expect a hard worker like this to rest on its laurels. It doesn't. After it snarls through a heavy work schedule, the Adventurer is ready to become its other self ... An on the town swinger ... when muscle plays second fiddle to sporty styling." (N Mort Collection)

The Adventurer interior came in two varieties. The Standard interior (shown) was vinyl with a fabric insert available in blue, green, black or tan bench seat. The full carpeting, textured fiberglass door trim panels and headliner were all color-keyed to match the seat. Always noted in the late sixties was the standard cigar lighter, which was a desirable option back then. (N Mort Collection)

No matter how you utilized your Adventurer, this ½-ton was up for it. For bigger or longer everyday loads you could order your D100 on a 128in wheelbase. A total of 13 exterior colors were offered – even in 1968 'Bright Turquoise' was still being offered. Some of the more popular options included power steering on V8 versions, two-tone paint, an anti-spin differential, a box-mounted spare tire carrier, tinted glass and an oil pressure gauge. (N Mort Collection)

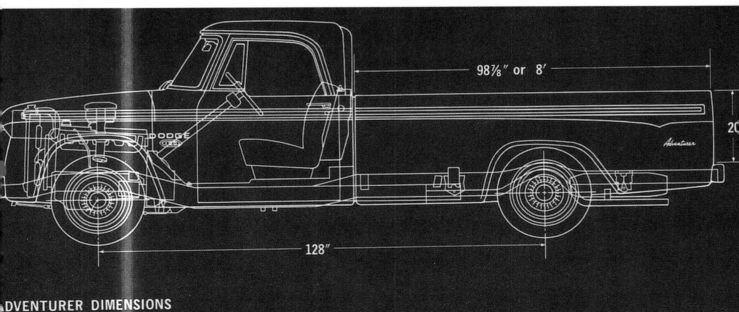

98⅞" or 8'

128"

ADVENTURER DIMENSIONS

Some of the more popular options included a box-mounted spare tire, power steering, two-tone paint, west coast mirrors, an oil pressure gauge and tinted glass.

The Adventurer model name would continue throughout the entire next decade.

1962 International C-99

The Canadian market has never been exactly the same as that of its US neighbor to the south. The northern climate, a population approximately one-tenth that of America, and generally a higher cost of living with lower wages, resulted in a population that bought far more lower-priced vehicles.

With Dodge, Chevrolet, Ford and even Studebaker all selling 'Compact' pickup ½-ton trucks in the form of the A100, Corvair 95, Econoline and Champ,

The C-99 International badge is rarely seen today. Fully chromed, it proudly announced the uniquely Canadian 'Compact' ½-ton pickup truck. (Courtesy Southland International)

The C-99 was conceived, designed and engineered in Canada by International Harvester Company of Canada Ltd in Hamilton, Ontario. (Courtesy Southland International)

As seen in this ¾ rearview, the C-99 had a full-size cab, but was fitted with an extra-short, 6ft version of the standard wide Bonus Load box on a smaller wheelbase. (Courtesy Southland International)

The 152ci, slant 4-cylinder engine was sourced from the smaller 4x4 Scout range, while the driveline and other suspension components were borrowed from the regular ½-ton pickup lines. (Courtesy Southland International)

The rear box was generous to the point that, when fully loaded to its 4000 GVW rating, the four-cylinder engine proved to be inadequate. The model was dropped in Canada in 1963, but suprisingly reappeared in the US in 1963 as the C-900. (Courtesy Southland International)

International came up with a distinctive Canadian-built model, dubbed the C-99. It was the lowest priced pickup truck on the market when unveiled in 1961.

Stylish enough and noted for its good handling, the C-99 proved to be somewhat sluggish in comparison to the more powerful competition, while its 16-22mpg fuel economy was disappointing. Yet, in comparison, its 4000lb GVW rating exceeded most of the full-size competition.

Inside, there was full instrumentation with no warning lights, and the door panels and the seat, with its striped insert, were outfitted in very basic, practical vinyl. Although pleasant and very functional, the engine noise, rattles, stiff suspension and short wheelbase made it rather tiring.

After two years it was dropped in Canada, but surprisingly reappeared in the United States as the C-900 model, which soldiered on until being unceremoniously dropped in 1969.

1965 Ford Mercury

In 1965 Ford introduced its 'Twin-I-Beam' independent front suspension on its F-Series trucks, which was

This fully restored 1965 Mercury Pickup was as much an attention getter when new as it is today. Its bright red and strong, contrasting white accent color scheme and added brightwork would easily draw potential buyers into the showroom. Just three years later in 1968, Ford of Canada ended all Mercury truck production. (Andrew Mort)

The Mercury script, badging, trim and grille design differed slightly from its Ford equivalent. (Andrew Mort)

naturally available on its Canadian-built Mercury versions. The unique to Ford suspension provided a smoother, more comfortable ride over all surfaces, compared to the old system. It was a rugged design that didn't require an extensive frame modification. It would prove worthy, and be a mainstay on Ford pickups for more than two decades. The Haltenberger steering linkage was also new.

93

A slightly different grille and relocation of the parking lights provided a fresh frontal appearance. A complete, from-the-ground-up, restoration and rebuild was completed on this Resto-Mod. Looking virtually stock, only its new aftermarket wheels shod in radial tires, and a new 'crate' factory motor are obvious modern updates. (Andrew Mort)

Both these engineering changes helped increase sales substantially to a record 563,137 light-duty truck sales in 1965.

Like its Ford sibling, visually little changed on the 115in wheelbase 1965 Mercury ½-ton pickup. Still, Mercury had its distinctive trim, colors and up-scale image, yet it was the three new engines that brought buyers into the showrooms. Standard power was the

Inside the period-like look continues with this 1965 Mercury's red and black patterned vinyl and cloth seat. The grey carpeting was added, and also concealed extra insulation for a quieter and cooler interior. A factory AM pushbutton radio sits in the fully refinished dash, and the original white, stylish deep-dish steering wheel was retained. Air-conditioning was available, and originally ordered for this truck. (Andrew Mort)

same 150hp, 240ci six-cylinder, but the 170hp, 300ci Six or the 208hp, 352ci V8 could provide more power.

The six-cylinder engines were robust with seven-main-bearing crankshafts and hydraulic lifters. The equally strong V8 would prove to be a long-term powerplant.

Inside, the Mercury version also got a redesigned

The make was obvious to those driving behind this Mercury pickup truck back in 1965. Although sometimes bought as a preference over the Ford equivalent, a lot of the time Canadian buyers bought a Mercury truck because it was the only Ford Motor Company dealership in their area.
(Andrew Mort)

instrument panel, similar to the Ford F-100, but with minor trim differences. The standard rubber floor mat was gone, replaced by a more durable vinyl. The interiors were also more colorful with a choice of red, green, blue, or tan to complement the exterior color.

1969 Chevrolet C10

By 1969 ½-ton pickup trucks were being used more and more for recreational use and personal transportation. As a result of this evolution in the market, the newest Chevrolet C10 was following the latest trends.

Exterior changes were kept to a minimum, but followed the styling cues in the industry towards bigger, bolder looks, with a more imposing grille and higher power-bulge hood line. The lighting and outside mirrors were improved. Two-toning was still a popular option.

As well as the popular Fleetside, Chevy still offered the rugged Stepside, which came with the same hood and grille. Short runningboards were still fitted between the cab and the rear fenders to assist in loading. The heavy-duty flared fenders were designed to provide additional strength and rigidity. Box width front-to-back was 50in, which was a mainstay measurement in the construction and home-building business for carrying

This 1969 Chevrolet C10 Custom Fleetside Pickup was originally sold in California. A rust-free example, it still has all of its original sheet metal. Note the all-new for 1969 grille. The base C10 models came with plain rubber window gaskets, no side trim, and painted bumpers and hubcaps. (Andrew Mort)

4x8ft plywood and drywall. The box floors were wood with steel skid strips for sliding cargo in and out.

There were demands from the campers, boat and trailer-towing crowd, as well as traditional buyers for more powerful engines with greater torque. At the same time, the younger generation wanted more horsepower for their 'Sport' trucks.

Chevy responded with its new 350ci V8 and a 4-bbl

All C10 Chevrolet pickups came standard with self-adjusting, four-wheel brakes, a dual master cylinder, and back-up lights, due to government regulations. A fresh oak plank bed floor was fitted on this nut and bolt restoration. (Andrew Mort)

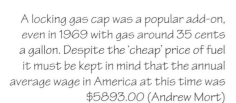

A locking gas cap was a popular add-on, even in 1969 with gas around 35 cents a gallon. Despite the 'cheap' price of fuel it must be kept in mind that the annual average wage in America at this time was $5893.00 (Andrew Mort)

The new for 1969 and soon-to-be legendarily reliable, 350ci V8 motor, was hooked-up to the optional Turbo Hydra-Matic automatic transmission. Horsepower on this example was boosted from the stock 280hp to 300hp. This 1969 short-box Chevrolet was also lowered, and featured upgraded power front disc brakes, fresh trim, and a new front and rear chrome bumper. (Andrew Mort)

The interior in this 1969 model has been somewhat upgraded, but new features for this year were a smaller-diameter steering wheel, redesigned seat, and the addition of a foot-operated hand-brake. Also featured here was the very desirable, factory-fitted air-conditioning and power steering option. (Andrew Mort)

310hp, 396ci V8. Power steering had been offered as an option, starting in 1968. Other improvements included an automatic choke on every engine, a new isolated, quieter steering shaft, and two-stage multi-leaf rear springs.

Inside were brighter interior colors and a quieter interior, due to improved door seals for a tighter fit.

Chevrolet and GMC would carry this handsome design into the mid-1970s.

Optional equipment on 1960s pickup trucks

In the last years of the 1960s, vinyl covered, or vinyl-look roofs became a popular fashion option. First seen on two-door hardtops to provide a convertible look, it quickly spread to two and four-door sedans, station wagons and even pickup trucks which often provided a more 'formal' as well as sporty look. Dodge and Fargo trucks lent themselves particularly well to vinyl, or in this case a crinkle painted black roof treatment. This look remained popular on American vehicles into the 1980s, despite continual problems of lifting and peeling vinyl, as well as rust.
(N Mort Collection)

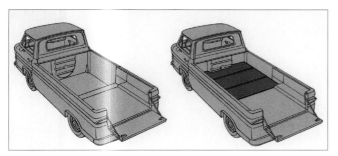

Perhaps the strangest option, rather than standard equipment, was the 'level load floor' accessory that provided a tailgate level flat floor on Chevrolet's Corvair 95 pickup box. It was constructed in three sections to permit partial use for special purposes or loads. (N Mort Collection)

In the 1960s, American manufacturers began to 'package' options in a bundle to provide better value – not to mention it being easier to build on a production line. Often the list of items in a package was extensive. For example, this 'Custom Cab Option' offered on the 1965 Jeep Gladiator included inside features, such as a color-keyed instrument panel and vinyl door panels, a cigar lighter, dual padded sunvisors, and left and right door armrests. Exterior features consisted of stainless steel rear cab, windscreen and door window moldings, and a chrome grille and front bumper.
(N Mort Collection)

The packaging of options normally included only a small number of upgrades. The packages varied from make to make and model to model, but were very obviously named for the instant recognition of buyers. This 1966 image features a 'Visibility Package' consisting of two-speed windscreen wipers, an inside non-glare mirror, and an outside remote-controlled mirror. Other packages evident are the 'Courtesy Light Package' which included an ashtray, glovebox and map light, and a 'Seat Package' featuring either just the bucket seats or the bucket seats with a console. (N Mort Collection)

Heavy-Duty Option Packages proved to be very popular on pickup trucks. For example, the Heavy-Duty Option Package on the Econoline E-100 could ostensibly turn this pickup into an easy ¾ to 1-ton hauler. The package featured the 170ci six-cylinder engine, new heavy-duty front and rear springs with a 955-1200lb capacity, respectively, heavier underbody construction, a 4.5:1 ratio rear axle with a 2700lb capacity and the ability to carry loads up to 2000lb in its 7ft long, 5ft wide and 2ft deep box. (N Mort Collection)

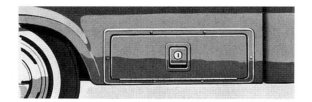

A novel idea that has been seen off and on pickup trucks right into the present millennium, is the built-in optional 'Tool Box.' On the 1964 Ford F-Series pickups the lockable box was located below the pickup box floor, just ahead of the right rear wheel, so as not to interfere with the cab or loadspace. The tool box lid was hinged and mounted flush with the pickup box for easy access. (N Mort Collection)

In 1960 in America only 20 percent of the vehicles manufactured were fitted with A/C. The Thermador Cooler was one of many add-on air-conditioning accessories still available in the 1960s. Not much had changed over the past 30 years, other than in the way the cooler held cold water or ice. Some coolers used cloth rolls that the passenger or driver could turn continually, to soak-up the cold water that the air passed over. Some even used shavings to hold the water. Eventually fans were added to force the cool air out even more. (N Mort Collection)

Air-conditioning was first offered by Packard in 1939 as an option, but in 1954 Nash offered its top-of-the-line Ambassador with the first front, fully integrated heating, ventilating, and air-conditioning system. American Motors Corporation made A/C standard on all its mid-priced Ambassador models in 1968, which helped motivate the competition to offer it on all its vehicles including trucks. By 1969 air-conditioning was being ordered on 54 percent of the vehicles purchased. No longer were the bulky, inefficient aftermarket, non-integrated air-conditioning systems required. Now, all vehicles, including trucks, had a factory designed, fully integrated system, such as the one pictured here in a 1968 Dodge D100. (N Mort Collection)

Whitewall tires continued to be offered as optional on ½-ton pickup trucks in the sixties, as seen on this 1961 Ford Styleside. It was noted in the advertisement, but whitewalls seem quite out of place on what is obviously a pickup used for work and everyday heavy loads. (N Mort Collection)

Side trim was often optional, but Ford went one step further in 1964, when it offered "optional full-length anodized side moldings." Anodizing increased resistance to wear or corrosion, and in the case of trim protected the painted emblems from any oxidation. (N Mort Collection)

By the same author –

Those were the days ...™

American ½-ton Pickup Trucks
of the 1950s

Examining the evolution of the popular ½-ton American pickup truck in the 1950s, from a basic utility vehicle, to stylish icon and North America's best selling vehicle, this volume focuses on specifications, rarer makes and models, industry facts and figures, and optional equipment, through detailed text and previously unpublished images.

ISBN: 978-1-845848-02-6
Paperback • 19x20.5cm • $25.95* USA /$30.95 CAN/£14.99* UK • 112 pages • 140 colour pictures

For more info on Veloce titles, visit our website at www.veloce.co.uk
• email: info@veloce.co.uk • Tel: +44(0)1305 260068
* prices subject to change, p&p extra

By the same author –

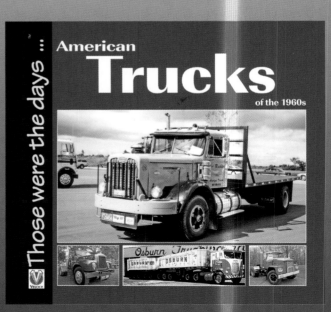

For more information on Veloce titles visit our website: **www.veloce.co.uk**

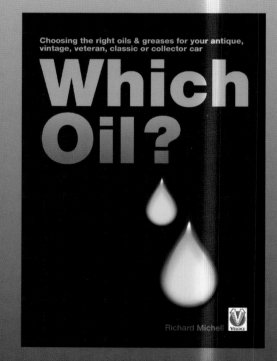

Index